"This book articulates thi words for, addressing the beautiful complexity of what drives us to create and what we encounter when we do."

—PATTI SMITH
acclaimed singer-songwriter and author

"In *The Discipline of Inspiration*, Carey Wallace embarks on a profound meditation on the creative process, blending art, spirituality, and discipline in a way that resonates with artists and seekers alike. Wallace examines the misunderstood nature of inspiration and the role of dedication in the act of creation. Drawing on insights from painters, poets, musicians, and thinkers across time, Wallace offers practical tools for finding our art and nurturing our creativity wherever we are—for that is the precise location of the mysterious force that guides us. Whether you're an artist or seeking a deeper understanding of the creative impulse, *The Discipline of Inspiration* wondrously unlocks the power of everyday inspiration, gratitude, and beauty."

—AIREA D. MATTHEWS
author of *Simulacra* and *Bread and Circus*,
codirector of the Bryn Mawr creative writing program

"Carey Wallace has subverted the (misbegotten) notion that 'inspiration' is too fickle and, perhaps, 'spiritualized' a tool for the artist to rely on. By wedding the practice of faith to the practice of artmaking, Wallace is helping reclaim the seemingly archaic notion of the Creator as the ultimate source of all creation. Drawing on classic spiritual disciplines like manual labor and poverty and fasting, Wallace offers surprising ways for contemporary art-makers to fashion lives devoted to their craft. She makes her case without antagonism or Christian triumphalism, but with the quiet certainty of one who has her spiritual game together. Her insights are clearly hard won, and her prose is as inspired as her subject."

—JOE HOOVER, SJ
poetry editor at *America*,
author of *O Death, Where Is Thy Sting? A Meditation on Suffering*

"As an artist and creator, I feel like I've been waiting for this book my whole life. Carey Wallace delves into the mystery behind the greatest motivation of life—inspiration—and gives us a poetic, expansive road map to guide us toward cultivating it in our own lives. This book is a real treasure."

—WAYNE ADAMS
multimedia artist,
former board chair of Christians in the Visual Arts

THE DISCIPLINE *of* INSPIRATION

The Mysterious Encounter *with* God *at the* Heart *of* Creativity

CAREY WALLACE

WILLIAM B. EERDMANS PUBLISHING COMPANY
GRAND RAPIDS, MICHIGAN

Wm. B. Eerdmans Publishing Co.
4035 Park East Court SE, Grand Rapids, Michigan 49546
www.eerdmans.com

© 2025 Carey Wallace
All rights reserved
Published 2025

Book design by Lydia Hall

Printed in the United States of America

31 30 29 28 27 26 25   1 2 3 4 5 6 7

ISBN 978-0-8028-8407-7

Library of Congress Cataloging-in-Publication Data

Names: Wallace, Carey, 1974– author.
Title: The discipline of inspiration : the mysterious encounter with
   God at the heart of creativity / Carey Wallace.
Description: Grand Rapids, Michigan : William B. Eerdmans Publishing Company, 2024. | Includes bibliographical references. | Summary: "Carey Wallace defines inspiration and offers practical strategies to help everyone find more of it"—Provided by publisher.
Identifiers: LCCN 2024002429 | ISBN 9780802884077 |
   ISBN 9781467468121 (epub)
Subjects: LCSH: Creative ability—Religious aspects—Christianity. |
   BISAC: RELIGION / Christianity / Literature & the Arts |
   PHILOSOPHY / Aesthetics
Classification: LCC BT709.5 .W36 2024 |
   DDC 248.4/9—dc23/eng/20240513
LC record available at https://lccn.loc.gov/2024002429

for my brother,
the artist

*Through him all things were made.
Without him, nothing was made that has been made.*

THE GOSPEL OF JOHN

CONTENTS

INTRODUCTION	1
The Core of Creation	3
Clues to Inspiration	6
BOOK ONE: INSPIRATION	13
The Discovery of Art	15
The Source of Inspiration	20
Not Everything Is Art	28
Art and Evil	34
The Territory of Imagination	39
Art and Worship	42
Who Is the Muse?	47
Art and Love	56

BOOK TWO: INCARNATION   59

The Mechanics of Incarnation	61
The Universal Voice	67
Incarnation and Audience	70
The Cascade of Incarnation	73
Incarnation and Difficulty	76
Incarnation in Culture	82
Incarnation and Imitation	85
Incarnation and Art	89
Incarnation and the Human Muse	93
The Paradox of Incarnation	99
The Self as Source	101
Incarnation and Technique	110
Incarnation and Discipline	114
The Myth of Work	117
Talent, Technique, and Inspiration	122
The Work of Art	129

BOOK THREE: DISCIPLINE   131

The Mechanics of Surrender	133
The Spiritual Disciplines	135
Rest	137
Silence	141
Solitude	143
Attention	145
Meditation	148

Manual Labor	150
Prayer	152
Gratitude	154
Poverty and Fasting	156
Community	161
Discernment	168
Obedience	173
Service	175
Discipline and Inspiration	178
The Discipline of Art	180
CONCLUSIONS	**183**
Everyone Is an Artist, Everything Is Art	185
The Great Artist	191
Notes	195

INTRODUCTION

THE CORE OF CREATION

We mistreat the word *inspiration* almost as much as the word *love*.

Travel ads promise inspiration for the whole family if we just pick the right beach. Sports figures thank their families for inspiring them to kick balls down a field. Real estate agents, software companies, and pho places all promise their products don't just provide shelter, tools, or food—they also come loaded with inspiration.

But what does *inspiration* actually mean?

In the art world, we often identify artists by talent: how easy it is for them to draw a face or sing in tune.

Then we train them in technique: the skill they develop by running scales or learning how to handle paint.

But even enormous amounts of talent and technique can add up to very little without a third element: inspiration.

Inspiration is what tells the painter what to paint and the singer how to sing.

It fuses talent and technique, and transfigures them into art.

To create, we need it more than either talent or technique. Even when we don't have much talent or technique, inspiration, on its own, can provoke strange and beautiful pieces.

But inspiration doesn't just speak in narrow categories of art. It speaks to all of us, in all kinds of places: in the impulse to throw some new spice into a meal, in the way we plant our backyard garden, in the stories we wish we knew how to tell, in the melodies we hear in our dreams—whether we would ever dare claim the name of artist for ourselves, or not.

The encounter with inspiration is the addictive core at the heart of creation.

We don't endure the work, doubt, and sacrifice of creation for applause, or prestige, or pay.

Because no praise or pay can compete with the reward of creation itself: the way time both expands and stops, the incomparable blend of freedom and possession, the total self-forgetfulness and the return to our true selves in the grip of inspiration.

In fact, for many artists, fame is a burden and pay an afterthought. The anxiety to "make it" doesn't stem from a lust for wealth or fame, but from our desire for more freedom to seek inspiration, and act on it.

The vast majority of teaching in the arts is devoted to technique: developing the technical skill to execute an artistic vision. Or taxonomy: how to identify and sort the products of creation.

That's because both technique and taxonomy lend themselves easily to academic discipline—the ordered syllabus, the predictable relationship between practice and skill. We teach what we can measure, and what we can reliably deliver.

If inspiration is discussed at all, the conversation usually happens outside class. Artists swap tricks during studio hours, pick up clues from offhand comments, look for patterns in our own experience: the way ideas often arrive in the shower, in conversation, just before sleep, the way a glance away from our work can set our stalled minds free to receive.

A professor tells a student to go for a walk when the ideas won't come.

An architect goes to bed, even in the middle of the day, when she's got a problem she can't solve.

Some people live a lifetime with inspiration that seems both unpredictable and ferocious.

Some suffer for years from inspiration's absence.

Some develop a wealth of experience with inspiration through consistent discipline.

But we often harbor a deep superstition that any attempt to understand inspiration might permanently disrupt its vital but mysterious machinery.

And another fear: perhaps that machinery can only operate in perfect obscurity.

Others hold inspiration in contempt, as the addiction of amateurs.

Or question whether it even exists.

But that chorus of denials only shows how many people have had the experience of inspiration, and how many of us are looking for ways to understand and negotiate with it.

CLUES TO INSPIRATION

The meditations on inspiration in this book first emerged when I created a program to help artists establish strong disciplines in the context of daily life.

I had just published my first book with a major publisher, so I had some time on my hands. And when I have time on my hands, I spend a lot of it encouraging other artists to make more art.

This may sound selfless, but actually it's greedy.

I'm someone whose life has been saved by art again and again, both at moments of terrible crisis, and in the drone of daily life, when art reminded me how much more it could mean to be alive.

I wasn't encouraging other people to create because I was a good person. I was doing it because I know how much I need what artists make, and because I believe I'm not alone in needing art that way.

I wanted to see everyone create more. But I was especially interested in the people I knew who had made wonderful things in the past, but were no longer creating anything—which describes a lot of people.

A heartbreakingly high percentage of art school graduates never create consistently again. And many more people who wouldn't dare call themselves artists long to create—but never do.

So I began with bribery.

I grew up in Michigan, where my family had a small cottage on a small lake, shared by the descendants of my great-grandfather. I could sign up to live at the place for a week each summer, so I did.

Then I invited friends to come out. I told them they could stay for free and I'd cook for them.

The cost of entry was that during the week, they had to make something.

By the time my first book came out, that retreat had been running for over ten years. It had grown from a handful of kids in Michigan to an international group of artists.

In a single week, my brother and I recorded an entire record on a studio he set up in the garage, and his buddy recorded an entire record on the same equipment, at night. Award-winning filmmakers parked cameras down by the water's edge in the dark, taking time-lapse shots of the shifting stars. I wrote the first pages of my first novel there, and the first pages of this book. Another friend finished a play that was produced the following year in New York.

But I also got a hard look at the limits of retreats and residencies. One of our friends was so moved by the experience of living full-time as an artist that he came back from the retreat and quit his job. But it was never a viable financial decision, and eventually he had to get another one. Many other people who came out struggled to find time to create once they got back home, or stopped creating at all.

Nobody ever funded our retreat, beyond the generosity of my family in sharing the place, and the money my brother and I pooled for groceries. But an enormous amount of the financial support given to artists to create new work comes in the form of retreats and residencies. As we saw, they can offer powerful benefits: space and concentration, community and cross-pollination. But they can also be hard to find and hard to get into, especially for people who are not already part of some in-group.

And even if you do get in, their format made them logistically impossible for people like me. I was working full-time in blue-collar jobs, as a waitress and a maid, so that I'd still have time in my daily life to write for two hours a day. I only got two weeks of vacation a year. It was impossible for me to take the three, or six, or eight weeks that were offered by various prestigious retreats. The retreats were ostensibly free, but travel to them often wasn't. Even more important, nobody offered to replace the lost income for me—income I absolutely needed.

And I was single at the time. For people with partners, children, or even pets, the logistics and burden of taking a residency are even more intense. But the cost of not taking part in residencies can also be high: because so much arts funding is funneled through them, they're one of the major ways that artists connect and form cohorts that allow them to rise.

But after running a residency for ten years, those concerns weren't my fundamental objection to the big machinery of residencies and retreats. My fundamental objection is that retreats are based on what I believe is a dangerous lie: that to create at our best, we have to leave our lives behind.

It's an idea that divorces artists from the wellspring of the communities that shape and support, frustrate and challenge us, communities that we need, and communities that need us. And the more deeply artists embrace the idea that we need to be separate or distant from our daily lives to create, the higher the chance that we will not create anything at all.

At the same time, I could see how my own habit of daily creation had led to the publication of my first book. When I started college, I knew I wanted to write. I also knew college would be hard, and I didn't want it to crowd my writing out. So I committed to writing for two hours a day, every weekday, and did that all four years. When I graduated, I never took a job that wouldn't allow me to spend those two hours writing. That was how I had learned how to write. And that's how I had written enough that anyone would be interested in buying it.

Not only that: I could see a habit of creation in the lives of all the artists I knew who were finding any kind of success. Not all the habits looked the same. Some of them wrote novels on their phones while commuting to work by train. Some of them worked all day, then spent an hour painting. Some of them you could never see on Saturdays, because they spent that day in the studio. But all of them had some kind of strong creative habit in the context of their daily lives.

Those habits allowed them to produce a body of work large enough to fill a novel or a gallery. But even more important, their habits gave them the freedom to create. They didn't have to wait for anyone to choose them or pay them money—or even attention—to make what they wanted to make.

And nobody could ever take that away from them.

I wanted to start a program that would help more people, from all backgrounds, in all art forms, unlock the power of strong creative habits. To create a program that wasn't just for a chosen few, or for people who could afford to spend their time making art instead of supporting themselves, but for everyone. To offer a tool that might even shift what voices we're lucky enough to listen to, what stories we know, what images we see.

I wanted the heart of the program to be creation and community, not abstract discussions on art. But I also wanted the program to be informed by the testimony of working artists across genres and throughout time.

So I did a deep dive into all the direct speech I could find by artists on art. I sifted through interviews, letters, and biographies, looking for light on a whole suite of topics.

The artist's character: do artists have to be selfish, wild, irrational?
The artist's life: do artists have to be unhappy?
The definition of art.
The purpose of art.
The source of art.

What I found was that a demoralizingly large amount of what artists have to say about art was simply gossip and backbiting.

Tchaikovsky calls Brahms a "giftless bastard." Titian says Tintoretto will never "be anything but a dauber." Renoir snipes that da Vinci "should have stuck to flying machines." Dali calls Cézanne "a catastrophe of awkwardness," compares Mondrian to a fart, and claims that Picasso only rose to prominence by "out-uglying" all his fellow painters. Virginia Woolf describes James Joyce's *Ulysses* as "a queasy undergraduate scratching his pimples." Frida Kahlo says she'd rather sit on the floor in the market of Toluca and sell tortillas than have anything more to do with the surrealists of Paris.

And when artists do talk about art, nobody agrees on anything.

Oscar Wilde claims the purpose of art is to conceal the artist, while F. Scott Fitzgerald says an artist's self is all they have to sell.

Fra Angelico says that art requires much calm, while van Gogh claims that he even reads the newspaper "with fury."

T. S. Eliot says that, for a poet, "there is no method but to be very intelligent." Borges says poetry has little to do with intelligence. And James McNeill Whistler says the vastest intelligence cannot bring art about.

All of this confusion is compounded by the fact that no one has more credibility than a great artist when they talk about art. If a Tolstoy or a Toni Morrison makes a claim about the definition of art, who else in the world has the authority to argue with them?

The conversation on art among artists, through history, sounds a lot like a schoolyard argument. Everyone talks at once. No one really expects anyone else to listen. All kinds of people make lazy or outrageous claims, or even tell dangerous lies, and nobody seems to mind.

A handful of helpful truths sometimes emerge from this melee. But they never coalesce into a coherent vision.

And without any general agreement on the deepest questions about art, the conversation devolves into one of the oldest games in human history: deciding who's in and who's out.

Too many of our conversations on art revolve around trying to decide what is and isn't art. Or who is or isn't an artist. Those questions get asked again and again, in the pages of the most prestigious magazines, and by kids running down each other's favorite bands on the street.

But trying to decide what is and isn't art is a fool's game, or a tyrant's. It looks backwards, to what has already been made, instead of forward, to what could be. It distracts or even paralyzes us, instead of setting us free to create.

Still, in that cacophony of competing opinions, I did find one strange, consistent point of agreement. Across thousands of years and in all genres, artists reached for the same language to describe the moment of inspiration.

Again and again, they describe the sensation that inspiration comes from something beyond them, a force or personality distinct from their own.

Something that draws things from them that they did not plan, that takes them in directions they had never imagined.

To create things that they can't believe they made.

Where do you get your inspiration?

Artists hear this question all the time.

Some of us respond with pat speeches. Some of us give the most sincere answers we can. Some of us lapse into sullen silence, because it's a question that makes it sound like creating art is mainly a matter of swiping ideas out of the air, which ignores the choices, and skill, and sacrifice art also requires.

But there's a deeper reason the question makes us uneasy: most of us don't know the answer.

And all of us are aware that anyone who asks has placed a finger squarely on the central moment in our lives as artists.

The insistent voice of inspiration is what first prompted us to create. It's why we've spent so much of our lives making things we may not ever be able to explain.

Without inspiration, we know that all our work and sacrifice may not amount to anything.

But we don't know where inspiration comes from.

We don't know why it arrives when it does, why it disappears, or what it means.

We don't understand its properties, its mechanics, its price.
And we are never sure where to go to get more.

But it is possible to think rigorously about inspiration: what it is, where it comes from, and what it might mean.

Exploring those questions can shed light on many others: the source of art, its purpose and definition.

It can point us to practical tools, to welcome more inspiration in both our work and our lives.

And an answer to that constant question, from the world and our own hearts: where do you get your inspiration?

BOOK ONE
INSPIRATION

All art comes from God.
    This is art's only source, and its only definition.
    For artists, the sense that art flows from something beyond our understanding or control is nothing new.
    It is the source of our best work and deepest fears.
    It is the site of our hardest-fought battles.
    It stands at the heart of our lives as artists.

THE DISCOVERY OF ART

The sensation that inspiration flows from something beyond us cuts across all genres and echoes through the ages.

The ancients created the muses to name the sensation, which Homer describes at the beginning of the *Odyssey*: "Tell me the story, muse . . . beginning wherever you will."

Most of the old gods are now retired or disguised, but our language is still full of traces of the sensation that inspiration flows into us from somewhere else.

We ask an artist where she "got" her ideas. We talk about how a writer "found" the words—as if those images and words exist already, somewhere else.

In many familiar phrases, the artist is passive but inspiration is active, sometimes to the point of violence: *it came to me, it hit me, it struck me.*

And artists both seek and complain about the moment when a piece takes on "a life of its own."

When artists describe creation, this language of discovery becomes even more striking.

Hoagy Carmichael, who wrote "Georgia on My Mind," "Stardust," and dozens of other jazz standards, says, "You don't write melodies, you find them." His description matches the Romantic composer Claude Debussy's, who worked almost a hundred years earlier, on another continent: "There is no theory. You only have to listen." And Debussy's explanation has something in common with the rapper Nas, who says: "I hear it, and my hand's too slow. That's been a big problem for me."

Four hundred years ago, Michelangelo described the same sense of discovery, despite the fact that he worked in a completely different genre, as a painter and sculptor. He writes in his sonnets that no artist can conceive of anything that is not already contained in a block of marble, which may be the seed of his very famous but possibly spurious bon mot: "I saw the angel in the marble, and carved until I set him free."

And two hundred years before Michelangelo, Dante, in his Divine Comedy, says that his poetry is not really authored by him but by Love, which dictates his poetry to something deep within him.

The sensation of discovery in creation persists even as modern life has dealt death blows to other mysteries.

"I don't think a writer should meddle too much with his own work," Borges, the giant of Argentine letters, said in 1967. "He should let the work write itself."

"The song will ultimately tell me what it wants," says the legendary Motown composer Lamont Dozier. "So I just have to have the patience to let it unfold. You discipline yourself and do the work . . . but then something greater takes over."

Patti Smith, poet and punk singer, describes photographer Robert Mapplethorpe's process in similar terms: "Most of the time, it seemed as if the piece was fully formed in his mind. . . . It was more a question of executing something he saw in a flash."

Sam Cooke describes a similar experience in writing one of the most important songs in the American songbook, "A Change Is Gonna Come." It was one of his most complex songs, but it arrived faster than anything else he ever wrote. "The song just came to me," he says. "I never scuffled with the words or anything. It was like it was somebody else's song."

Carole King describes the same sensation when writing "You've Got a Friend": "The song wrote itself. It was written by something outside of myself through me."

Novelist Toni Morrison says that the key to creation is "being open—not scratching for it, not digging for it, not constructing something, but being open to the situation and trusting that what you don't know will be available to you. It is bigger than your overt consciousness or your intelligence or even your gifts; it is out there somewhere, and you have to let it in."

The writer Sherman Alexie describes a similar experience through the thoughts of a character who is also a writer: "Thomas looked into himself. He knew his stories came from beyond his body and mind, beyond his tiny soul."

Sometimes inspiration seems to come from so far beyond an artist that the artist barely recognizes their own work. Novelist Eudora Welty says that reading proofs of her novels came as a "real shock . . . I didn't write this."

"If a writer is any good," her fellow author Flannery O'Connor adds, ". . . it will always be a greater surprise to him than it can ever be to his reader."

Ernest Hemingway describes the same sensation, through the voice of an autobiographical character: "When I read it I would think this is so good I couldn't have written it. I must have read it somewhere. Probably in the *Saturday Evening Post*."

Songwriter Paul Simon's sense of surprise at his work is so profound that he actually thinks of himself as part of his own audience. "I'm interested in what I find, as opposed to what I'm planning," he says. "I like to be the audience, too . . . to discover it rather than plot it out. That's the feeling . . . that you're a transmitter. It comes through you. But you don't possess it. You can't control it or dictate to it. You're just waiting . . . waiting for the show to begin."

Fernando Pessoa, one of Portugal's foundational writers, goes so far as to say that his work has absolutely nothing to do with him: "Neither this work nor those to follow have anything to do with the man who writes them. He doesn't agree or disagree with what's in them. He writes as if he were being dictated to. And as if the person dictating were a friend (and for that reason could freely ask him to write down what he dictates), the writer finds the dictation interesting, perhaps just out of friendship."

Poet Lucille Clifton was known for using similar language to describe her process, saying that something in her knew how to write poetry better than she did.

Poet Kamilah Aisha Moon puts it even more simply: "I readily acknowledge that I am an instrument of spirit."

The iconic songwriter and performer Beyonce Knowles-Carter is familiar with the same contrast between her voice and the voice of inspiration—even when they both come from her own mouth. The difference between her on-stage and off-stage personas is so complete that she's given her on-stage alter ego a name of her own: Sasha Fierce. "It's like a blackout, when I'm onstage," she says. "I don't know what . . . happens. I am gone."

Artists don't just describe inspiration as an element that comes from beyond them. They also describe it as having a will of its own—a will that's often at odds with theirs.

"I have written the poems from immediate dictation," William Blake writes about his poem cycle *Milton and Jerusalem*, "without premeditation and even against my will."

"I didn't want to write it," songwriter John Lennon says of his song, "Across the Universe." "It wrote itself. It drove me out of bed. I was just slightly irritable and I went downstairs and I couldn't get to sleep until I put it on paper."

"If I exhaust my will enough to get tired of wanting to be somebody," says poet Marie Howe, "occasionally something can happen that I want to read—so that you're really seeing this thing that's trying to speak through you. The hardest thing is to give up what we were trying to say and let whatever speaks say us."

The impulses of inspiration may even be at odds with the artist's conscious creed. Despite his "pessimistic, nihilistic actions and assertions," artist Gerhard Richter says, his work has the sole aim of "creating or discovering hope . . . that something is going to come, which I do not know, which I have been unable to plan, which is better and wiser than I am, and which is also more universal."

Songwriter Tom Waits even tells a story of talking back to inspiration, while driving down a freeway with a melody in his head and no way to write it down: "Excuse me, can you not see that I'm driving? If you really want to exist, come back at a more opportune moment. Otherwise, go bother somebody else today. Go bother Leonard Cohen."

This is another trait of inspiration: many artists feel like it seeks entry to the world through anyone who will respond to it. "Songwriting is like fishing in a stream," Arlo Guthrie says. "You put in your line and hope you catch something. And I don't think anyone downstream from Bob Dylan ever caught anything."

Writer Anne Lamott phrases this same idea both as advice, and as a threat: "Carry a pen at all times, or God will give me all the great lines and images that were supposed to be yours, because I always have a pen."

It's a threat Michael Jackson took seriously. Before his last planned tour, he recorded feverishly, insisting that a higher power dictated the songs.

Worried about his health, a friend suggested that Jackson ask the higher power to give him the songs *after* the tour.

"I can't," Jackson answered. "Then he might give them to Prince."

THE SOURCE OF INSPIRATION

Artists are in almost eerie agreement about the sensation of inspiration.

But they offer wildly different explanations as to where it comes from.

The invention of the unconscious offered one major possibility.

Early surrealists were quick to make the connection between the alienation they felt at the moment of inspiration, and this hidden quadrant of the mind.

Inspiration didn't flow from any external muse, they began to argue. It flowed from a core of impressions buried in their own brains, a position many other artists have taken since then.

"We carry thousands of years of . . . blood and memory," says dancer and choreographer Martha Graham. "How else to explain those instinctive gestures and thoughts that come to us, with little preparation or expectation?"

Paul Simon explains his sense of surprise at his own work the same way. It comes from the "subconscious," he says. "Unless you believe that someone is sending you a signal from another planet or another sphere. I don't think that way."

Poet Wallace Stevens is even more unequivocal: "No longer do I believe that there is a mystic muse, sister of the Minotaur. This is another of the monsters I had for nurse, whom I have wasted. I am myself a part of what is real, and it is my own speech and the strength of it, this only, that I hear or ever shall."

To explain inspiration as a product of the unconscious holds some obvious attractions for an artist.

First, it's wonderfully flattering. Under this theory, an artist is no longer the victim or devotee of a mysterious external force. Instead, we are the absolute author of all our work.

Not only that, but the elements in our work that seem foreign to us—better, wiser, fiercer, stronger than our own thoughts or life—no longer expose our limits. Instead, they reveal our hidden strengths, a glimpse into our rich inner worlds.

This explanation also matches our experience. The voice of inspiration speaks within us. We have built no machines yet that can measure any other origin. A scientific age must always choose the simplest explanation. If the voice speaks inside us, that is where it must come from.

But often, what's most remarkable about a work of art is not how fully it expresses the artist, but how fully it transcends the artist's limits, weakness, and prejudice.

The film *Amadeus* gives a remarkably clear illustration of the sometimes jarring, sometimes heartbreaking disparity between an artist and their work. As played by Tom Hulce, the composer Mozart is frivolous, thoughtless, childish. His work is subtle, reflective, epic.

Although the film may have done a disservice to the historical Mozart, we don't have to look far to find examples of artists whose personal lives show little to no trace of the wisdom, compassion, and beauty that permeate their work. And on the flip side, we can all name artists with great personal charm or empathy whose work never lives up to their own best qualities.

The theory that inspiration is only a product of the unconscious is also called into question by other artifacts of the unconscious, like dreams.

Dreaming and creation are often linked in the popular mind. But in practice they are radically different experiences.

Dreams are sometimes vivid. But they are also irrational, disjointed, and vague. In contrast, inspiration is marked by a heightened, sometimes painful, clarity.

In dreams, the unconscious recombines elements of our lives with narrative patches, in an attempt to create a cohesive story. But dreams bear almost no resemblance to the narratives of great plays or novels—even when those pieces of art are trying to imitate dreams. Dreams and literature are so different that it's difficult to believe that they could be products of the same "author."

And many art works, especially in music and the visual arts, have no narrative at all, which makes it even more difficult to explain them as simply a by-product of the mind's attempts to explain life to itself.

Many artists are skeptical of the claim that inspiration is a product of the unconscious mind. "I dislike learned talk about 'the unconscious,' which always seems to imply that the very intelligent are able somehow to know what they don't know," writes poet Wendell Berry. "Much of what I have written has taken me by surprise. What I know does not yield a full or adequate accounting for what I have imagined. It seems to have been 'given.' My experience has taught me to believe in inspiration, about which I think nobody can speak with much authority."

Rapper Tupac Shakur offers a different explanation for the source of inspiration: it comes from spirits who have passed beyond this earth. "We ain't even really rapping," he says. "We're just letting our dead homies tell stories through us."

At least one artist has explained the sense that art flows from a source alien to the artist by ascribing it to actual aliens. Early rockabilly star Billy Lee Riley claimed that "rock 'n' roll was so strange that it had to come from Mars," and that "the little green men" taught him how to do the bop.

And many artists, both inside and outside traditional religious structures, describe inspiration as an encounter with God.

Songwriters as diverse as Brian Wilson, Carole King, Burt Bacharach, and Lamont Dozier all name God as the source of their inspiration, along with Jimmy Webb, who says, "I believe that He's the author of all this stuff," and Marvin Gaye, who told Smokey Robinson that his classic album *What's Going On* "wasn't done by me, Smoke. It was done by God." Robinson himself described his own songwriting as a gift from God, and Aretha Franklin called her singing "the gift that God gave me."

Harold Arlen remembers "Somewhere Over the Rainbow," one of the world's most-recorded songs, coming to him in a flash while he was headed to a movie: "It was as if the Lord said, 'Well, here it is, now stop worrying about it!'"

Jazz trumpeter Ornette Coleman also points to the divine as the source of art: "Ideas reside in the same place as prayers."

"This is what God has created me to be," rapper DMX told his former wife Tashera Simmons shortly before he died. "I'm a vessel for the world."

And Rick Rubin, legendary producer and cofounder of Def Jam Records, believes that he makes art "as an offering to God."

The poet Rainer Maria Rilke actually addresses his observations about inspiration directly to God: "I wrote at Thy command, and knew not what I wrote."

It's an echo of poet Elizabeth Barrett Browning in "Aurora Leigh," who says that the instant we say a true word, we realize it is God's, not ours.

Anne Sexton describes the same sensation, a century later: "I had a kind of feeling Christ was speaking to me and telling me to write that story . . . the story he hadn't written."

The sensation that a spirit beyond ours is present at the moment of creation persists across continents and culture. Werner Herzog's *Cave of Forgotten Dreams* includes an account of an ethnographer traveling with an indigenous guide in northern Australia who begins to touch up an ancient rock painting in a stone shelter where they have stopped. When the ethnographer asks the guide about his work, the guide answers: "I am not painting. That is the hand of the spirit who is actually painting."

His reply is like a line the painter Henri Matisse wrote to the priest and famed designer of stained glass, Marie-Alain Couturier: "God held my hand. What could I do but obey?"

Some artists are satisfied to leave the identity of inspiration a mystery. "It's much like the life of a Catholic nun," says Leonard Cohen. "You're married to a mystery."

And even artists who work as closely as two members of a songwriting team may come to radically different conclusions. "Carole says they come from God," says King's longtime collaborator Gerry Goffin. "But I'm not that pretentious to think that God's gonna send me a lyric."

Goffin rejects the idea out of humility. Others reject it from rational skepticism. "Where they come from," says Hal David, Burt Bacharach's writing partner, "I don't know. A thousand years from now, some medical science will figure out where creative ideas come from. It's in the subconscious somewhere. It's in the mind somewhere."

We may not have to wait a thousand years. Modern neuroscientists have begun to map the activity of inspiration, name the implicated chemicals, push pins into the hidden quadrants of our minds. Psychologists have identified some of inspiration's visible triggers: nature, drugs, grief, discipline, rest, surprise. Titans of industry interested in potential profits from new ideas now run their own more-or-less scientific experiments to bolster creativity among their workers, with everything from snack bars to rock concerts to nap pods.

Science today knows more than it ever has about the neighborhood of inspiration in the mind and the external conditions that cultivate it. But many of the scientific advances of the past decades have only served to underscore how much we still don't know, and how uncertain what we do know is.

As electron microscopes and supercolliders allow us to break open and peer through the atom, we've discovered that, at the most granular level we can perceive, the most basic laws of classic physics seem to warp: matter is actually energy, light is both particle and wave. Over half the universe is indiscernible to any of our senses. Chaos pervades the entire system. And when we are able to observe, the simple fact that we watch changes the outcome.

Modern science has tamed electricity, put humans on the moon, and wiped entire diseases from the earth. It will no doubt continue to build on its already remarkable accomplishments. And it's possible that scientists in the future will come to empirically provable conclusions about the smallest units of matter—or the human mind.

But it's also possible that, when science finally does lay any of these areas bare, we may discover that empirical tests are not sufficient to observe, let alone understand, all things.

Despite all our advances, many territories of the mind are still a mystery. And the mind is not a closed system. New things flow into it all the time. Chemicals flood the brain at the sight of a loved one, a barking dog, a glass of wine—and with the changing tides of our own thoughts, which can generate responses of fear and love even when threats or lovers aren't actually there.

In identical environments, different minds will accept or ignore radically different facts and impressions. At the same party, one person will count the signs of wealth while another is distracted by the beautiful people. One person's attention will be drawn to laughter, another's to conflict. One will judge strangers by guessing their status, another based on their charisma or kindness.

And much of what each mind chooses to absorb, it also transforms. Our perceptions of reality are skewed by our culture, our beliefs, our prejudices. And every time we access a memory, we change it.

So at this moment, the appeal to the unconscious requires just as large a leap of faith as a full retreat into mystery. Certain areas of the brain light up at certain stimuli, so we can make educated guesses about which regions control hunger and attraction, memory or abstract thought. But we don't have the tools to catalog the mind, or whatever hidden structures would recombine and extrude its elements as the apocalypses of Bosch, or the Temptations' "Just My Imagination."

In fact, we may attribute inspiration to the unconscious precisely because the unconscious remains so impenetrable. It's become a catch-all for human behaviors and capabilities that seem beyond rational explanation: a safe place for an enlightened person to stash a mystery, while still keeping their self-respect as a modern thinker.

At some future point, we may produce far more accurate maps of the mind, and even decode the meaning of each tiny charge that leaps from synapse to synapse. But because our minds are susceptible to things beyond them, we will never be able to definitively establish what stimuli cause our mind's responses: an event in the visible world, a change in the weather of our own thoughts—or some signal that operates in a range currently outside measurable perception: what poets call muse, and prophets call God.

Even when each neuron is mapped, every chemical bottled, all dreams photographed, it will never be possible to prove that the unmeasurable presence of God is the fundamental ingredient in all art—just as it will never be possible to prove that it is not.

The more familiar we become with inspiration, the greater our sense that it operates beyond our control. No amount of technique, talent, or discipline can summon inspiration—or replace it.

It will not speak or roll over on command. It is not interested in any trade we offer or threats we make, either against it or ourselves.

That's because inspiration is not a resource like water or gold, or a creature we can hunt. <u>Inspiration is an intrusion of God into the world.</u>

<u>The search for inspiration is a species of prayer: an attempt to connect</u> with a force not just beyond ourselves, but beyond the <u>seen world.</u>

And art is a form of worship: the artist's reaction to the living presence of God.

Art is evidence of God's presence, and continually invokes it. It confounds some and enrages others, as God does. It comforts and heals, as God does. It chides and sears, as God does. It dazzles and quiets us, as God does. It bears witness, as God does. It appears in different guises to different people, as God does. It both reveals our weakness and returns us to our better selves, as God does.

It cannot be defined, as God cannot be defined.

It cannot be boxed, as God cannot be boxed.

It cannot be stopped, as God cannot be stopped.

Art is God's constant continuation of the original creation, through the hands and minds of humankind.

NOT EVERYTHING IS ART

The most obvious objection to this view of inspiration is mockery: did *God* inspire this violent movie, this misogynistic novel, this annoying but unforgettable Broadway chorus?

But not all cultural products are art.

Any form art takes—song, image, movement, word—can also be used in the service of propaganda, pornography, or entertainment—or various blends of them all.

Propaganda is created to make a point. We recognize it easily in fascist ceremonies and moralizing children's books. But propaganda doesn't just shore up philosophies and governments. It marks any work created to promote any point of view. A novel written to infect readers with the author's personal despair is only an inversion of a dictator's claims of false paradise. Both are forms of propaganda, just with different aims.

An enormous amount of propaganda in art is simply propaganda for the artist themselves: blazing guitar solos that do nothing for a song other than show off the player's chops, dazzling verbal flourishes that showcase an author's skill but distract from the story. Artists also create propaganda to build their own personal mythology: to replace the reality of their lives with a fiction of their own, in their own mind or the minds of others.

Some propaganda may even be inadvertent. The artist may sincerely believe, or want to believe, the point they make—the coward who writes tales of heroism, the philanderer who sings promises of eternal love, the alcoholic who paints pictures of a perfect world, free from disorder or pain.

These artists may be the first victims of their own propaganda. Their need to believe may help them to create especially potent lies. Recording those lies may reveal fundamental truths about human nature and desire. And the artist's sincerity may have a ring of authenticity that gives the propaganda added power.

But sincerity is not truth. And artists who are unable or unwilling to confront the deepest realities, either about ourselves or the world, will not produce art but propaganda, no matter how deeply felt.

Propaganda appears not just in campaign posters and parades, but everywhere from Hollywood movies to literary novels, in rap and country songs, in art flicks and fashion spreads.

It may be ingenious, even beautiful. But no matter how well-executed, and regardless of the cause it champions, its primary purpose is not to reveal, but convince.

Pornography makes promises it can't keep, not just about the body, but about food, comfort, freedom, violence, beauty, money, power. It pretends to expose a world that in fact does not exist: tailored to our desires and under our control.

By definition, pornography is never the thing itself. As long as we hold it in our hands, we can never actually grasp whatever it promises.

And pornography isn't found only in the dark swamps of the internet or on the racks at the back of drug stores. Almost all mainstream culture is full of it. It doesn't show up just in the mild, obvious titillation of revealing costumes and cheap sex. It's far more insidious in all the depictions of a world in which everything is brighter and more expensive than our own, everyone is smarter, funnier, better looking, and easier to categorize, and where events happen faster, make more sense, and settle more quickly into comforting resolutions.

This is not to say that anything beyond a strict adherence to reality constitutes pornography. All art chooses, focuses, and alters elements of life. And some artists meticulously craft impossible worlds that reveal, critique, or celebrate the best of our own.

But the perfectly lit, sanitary industry standards of commercial imagery and storytelling produce a counterfeit of life that's close enough to the real thing that we can take refuge in it from the genuine wisdom real life might otherwise teach us. This creates a pornography of life itself that is in many ways more dangerous than its brown-paper-wrapped cousin, which is at least honest in its aims.

Entertainment is a narcotic. It takes the form of circus clowns, acrobats, nonsense rhymes, magic tricks, telenovela plots, infectious beats. Entertainment distracts us from reality, lifts worry, breaks our awareness of the relentless flow of time, and offers unearned joy, laughter, pleasure, shock, and wonder.

Just like any other drug, it can be a gift or a thief. It can release us from pain, sometimes for long enough that we begin to heal. It can relieve our worries or shrink them to manageable size, so that we are able to think. It can remind us of the taste of hope, or simply how to laugh. But taken too long, or in excessive doses, it can blunt our minds, divorce us from real life, and permanently twist our vision.

By far the largest category of cultural production is failure: it doesn't work as anything, not even propaganda or pornography.

But all failure is not waste.

In experiment and practice the goal is to grow, not just succeed. And every new work, since it has never been made before, carries the threat of failure—otherwise it would be imitation, not art. If we never fail, it may be a sign that we never take the real risks art requires.

Failure can also serve as a lesson in craft. When work fails, as craftspeople we can inspect the machine, climb around on the hidden beams, fill our kits with new tools. We can learn the power of imperfection—missed notes that suddenly transform an entire piece, stray lines that point the way to a whole new story. And when we learn to recognize the telltale signs of failure—in our own work or the work of others—we can change tack more quickly when it appears, cut it out, or avoid it altogether.

Almost none of these categories—pornography, propaganda, and entertainment—ever appear unalloyed. Beautiful melodies are paired with empty, false, or even vicious lyrics. An actor's charisma shines through a weak script. Obscene lies are told in scenes of great beauty, and great truths are encrusted with profanity.

Even work produced with a single definite aim may unintentionally drift between categories. Propaganda may accidentally tell the truth. Pornography may unintentionally celebrate the object it set out to exploit. Military parades sometimes achieve moments of striking beauty. Jokes sometimes deliver profound insight.

And these categories of art, entertainment, pornography, and propaganda do not map reliably into categories of "high" and "low" art. Some rarefied theater productions contain nothing but banal prattle, while some pop songs offer indelible observations on the human condition. Television advertisements sometimes create wildly original visual experiences, while vaunted fine artists fill ostensibly important galleries with cynically derivative work.

And these categories are not just tangled or alloyed in every piece of work, but in the heart and mind of every artist. No artist, however great, produces only art. And any artist with the talent to create art likely has the facility to produce any other product in their genre. William Faulkner and F. Scott Fitzgerald wrote Hollywood thrillers. Andy Warhol drew advertisements.

That same facility can also allow an artist to mimic whatever style is currently in vogue in their contemporary art world. Savvy mimicry of contemporary styles can pass successfully for art, even for an entire career. And some artists don't copy the work of others, but the genuine inspiration that appeared in their own work, in earlier years.

We can see this constant flux between categories with frustration, that there is so little pure art in the world.

Or we can see it with hope, that art continues to emerge in the midst of failure and chaos.

The question of what is and is not art is complicated by the fact that art does not operate independent of an audience. Art is only ever completed in the mind of another human being.

In many ways, all people are disturbingly similar. But we are also, in ways that are just as significant, wildly different. Where one person sees pornography, another may see beauty. Where one finds despair, another may find truth. Music that one person hears as incitement to violence may serve another person as a safe release for rage. What seems like sentimental drivel to one may provide genuine comfort to another.

No piece of art, no matter how great, will move every audience. Even pieces very few people would define as art may have incredible meaning to someone—not just personal significance, but the significance of true art: to illuminate, transfigure, challenge and heal.

And despite all the time we spend and ink we spill arguing about what is and isn't art, the person who sees more art in the world, rather than less, is the luckier one.

Art itself both encompasses and inverts all the categories that compete with or masquerade as art.

Like propaganda, art has the power to change minds, but by revelation, not persuasion.

Like entertainment, art distracts us from this world, not by temporary illusion, but with a greater truth.

Pornography creates hunger without offering food. Art satisfies our hunger despite the fact that we haven't eaten. Pornography strips its objects of their true identity. Art invests its elements with resonance and weight far beyond their ordinary use.

As artists, we may never know with absolute certainty whether or not we have created art. Contemporary critics often look like fools in the light of history, and history itself is fickle. Aesthetic theories contradict each other and shift like tides.

The line where art begins and ends can be unclear even in the artist's own mind. We're never sure exactly when we've crossed into that territory, at what point we crossed back, or how to get there again.

Our confusion is often compounded by self-doubt that prevents us from recognizing our own triumphs. Or self-deception that keeps us from admitting our own failures. Or both.

Despite all this, in our best or most defenseless moments, we do know, deep in our hearts, both when we have created art, and when we have not.

We know it beyond rational thought, where art itself operates.

And the key to recognizing art is the same as the key to creating it: the courage to act on what we know, despite the fact that we may never be able to prove it.

ART AND EVIL

The idea that art comes from God raises another question: why does it emerge in bad places, and through bad people?

It's a concern that's especially urgent when art appears amid unquestionable evil or oppression: music played to accompany the sale of women and the nurture of addiction, buildings built to display excessive wealth or consolidate illegitimate power, the lust of Nazi officials for looted artworks even as they oversaw genocide on an industrial scale, the drawings one of America's most prolific serial killers created to help police identify his victims—because he was also a gifted artist.

But we also face it every time we learn about a favorite artist's weak, selfish, or even monstrous behavior.

The problem with this question is the assumptions it hides.

The first assumption is that God's main concern is morality.

It's an impression that's often encouraged by religious authorities, because systems of morality are easier to understand and enforce than encounters with a living God.

But the life of Jesus describes a God who seeks to meet us, even at great cost, despite our moral failures and in the midst of them.

And this principle holds true both in our lives, and in our art.

The second assumption is that we are capable of telling good from evil—and that we stand on the side of good.

But good and evil, strength and weakness, are inextricably bound in all our hearts.

If art could only be made by perfect people, there would be no art.

Many faiths assert that God is everywhere, at work amidst all things.

In practice, however, many of us think and act as if God is with us and our people, and not with *them*, whoever *they* are: rich or poor, women or men, these people or those people, sinners, heretics, or hypocrites.

But the most vibrant art often emerges among the rejected, the forgotten, the outcast. This is a sign that God is present in all places, and that God abandons no one.

Jesus was reviled by religious authorities for the company he kept. It should come as no surprise that God's creative spirit would continue to break out among the world's oppressed and outcast.

Or that, when other avenues to God are closed, the wounded and rejected, still thirsting for God, would seek an encounter with God in art.

Our choices matter—to us, to those we love, and to the world—but they cannot banish God, either from our own life, or from the lives of others.

[margin note: hidden or unhidden, God is present. Jung]

This is why the wounded, the rejected, and the outcast flock to the arts, both as creators and consumers: because there is a living God in art, who speaks to everyone, about everything.

Throughout history, religious authorities have been among the first to recognize the power of that living spirit in art.

But often, they have identified it as "the devil."

And they've used that claim to suppress art from Ovid to the Beatles, condemning what they can't control and don't yet understand.

Some artists do seek inspiration in the occult. In a series of séances, Victor Hugo engaged in hundreds of conversations with what he believed to be spirits while writing *Les Misérables*. And the legend of bluesman Robert Johnson exchanging his soul for his skill at a Delta crossroads is almost certainly false, but it's the perfect distillation of the myth that art can flow straight from a deal with the devil.

But evil has no power to create.

It can only twist, destroy, lie, or imitate, never make.

Creation is the act of God. It's a sign of God's presence, wherever it appears—no matter what we find around it, and whether anyone recognizes God's presence there, or not.

The presence of God often reveals what is concealed: beauty, power, and worth in things we might otherwise pass by—and evil we wish we could hide or ignore. So we can expect true art to lead us into confrontations with evil, both in the world and in ourselves. When art reckons with evil, it has incredible power. Through art, we can see the truth about evil, or tell it, without actually doing evil or being harmed by it.

But any work that confronts evil runs the risk of being deemed evil itself. Socially acceptable culture tends to gloss over evil: its prevalence, its variety, its strength, and its consequences. But that "safe," sanitized culture may tell the most dangerous lie: that evil is not powerful, or real.

Some artists do produce work that celebrates or advocates evil. And we all bear the responsibility to name and resist evil when we see it, in life and in art.

Our individual tolerances may also vary. Some people are far more sensitive to violence, flesh, or even despair than others. We all carry different wounds. So we may choose not to immerse ourselves in certain pieces for personal reasons.

But the most powerful position is not to discard any work of art as pure evil, but to offer the worship art elicits to God, even in the presence of evil. And to thank God for everything about a work that is good: the harmony of the music, the skill of the performers, the logic of the rhymes, the beauty of the image.

The fact that art flows into the world through imperfect people is a clear example of God's grace, giving good things where they have not been earned.

But it also reveals the potential for good—or greatness—that lies hidden in all of us.

The pop star posing like an icon on the cover of a magazine may actually be riddled with insecurity. The actor who brings us to tears with a soliloquy on friendship may actually be selfish and lonely.

But when they create something better than they can live up to, they are not lying about themselves, or the world. They've managed, in those moments, to welcome something that transcends their own lives and limits.

The dissonance between an artist's life and art can be sickening: beautiful melodies by an artist who engaged in incest or pedophilia, timeless truths written by an artist who actively supported a regime that destroyed cultures and oppressed millions.

Offering thanks to God for art, despite an artist's failings, allows us to navigate this vertigo.

We can clearly name an artist's failings, without discarding their art, or denying its power.

We aren't tempted to make excuses for an artist's life, simply because we see the value of their art.

To find God among all things, and not cower at any hint of evil, is the act of greatest faith.

To thank God for the beauty of the foulest propaganda undermines that propaganda in the most fundamental way.

To see the image of God in every person, no matter how difficult or depraved, strikes a blow against that depravity, and may even open a way out of it.

The great spiritual truth is not a set of instructions on how to keep our hands clean.

It's the stubborn presence of God with us, among broken and evil things.

THE TERRITORY OF IMAGINATION

Ironically, one of the primary enemies of the idea that art comes from God has been religion.
 Some of the friction between art and religion is superficial. Religion sometimes defines art as pornographic or blasphemous. The art world sometimes defines pornography or propaganda as art. Both sides object, with good reason.
 But the root cause of the conflict between art and religion lies much deeper.
 The fundamental problem is that art and faith both operate in the same territory of the mind.

Faith requires a virtuosic act of imagination from any believer. They must believe more in a world they have never seen than in the only one they have ever known. They must take action, not based on what they can see or hear, but what they believe about this unseen world.
 Faith depends on the same mechanism of the mind that makes art possible: the power of imagination that allows us to see a face in some daubs of paint, accept that a man dressed in mangy furs is a lion for the duration of a play, or gasp at a fistfight that is really nothing more than a handful of words on a page.

But art and religion make radically different claims about what happens in the moment we surrender to them.

Religion claims to bring us into contact with the only reality, one that holds a higher claim on our allegiance than any other loyalty or authority.

Art may convey great truths. And it often takes itself too seriously. But in the end, art insists that it is really nothing but a story, a picture, a show. No artist would want to be tried for the crimes they invent or act out.

But religion and art make false claims, on both sides.

Religion denies the fact that it depends on faith. It demands a place at the top of the world's hierarchies, rather than upending or transcending them. It denies the mystery and uncertainty that the existence of any realm beyond our own creates. Or it makes the absurd attempt to bind this transcendent mystery with the clumsy tools of this world's language, logic, or laws. It pretends to be a system of rules by which we can earn a certain outcome, rather than a means of surrender to an untamable God. In fact, the animosity of religion toward art has a great deal in common with the animosity of religious authority to the wildness and profligacy of a living God.

Art, on the other hand, denies the seriousness of its own consequences. An actor playing a murderous king may not be guilty of the carnage he portrays on stage, but the power of art can cut deeper than physical violence. It rewires our minds and reorganizes our hearts. To claim that it is *just* a song or *just* a show is a wild misstatement, if not a cynical lie.

Religion is terrified that if it acknowledges the role imagination plays in belief, religion itself will be reduced to nothing more than story or theater, a matter of smoke, mirrors, costumes and greasepaint.

But art may be the only language capable of grappling with religion's central concerns of truth and transcendence.

Public speech is always polluted by irony, power, and commerce, from the elaborate courtly vocabulary of previous centuries, to the promises of today's advertising and politics, which are so compromised that they don't even function as lies, since no one believes them in the first place.

We no longer believe our politicians, journalists, advertisements—or each other on social media. We're even more suspicious of religious leaders.

Art is the last language in which we can speak without cynicism about our hunger for faith and meaning, our deep sense of right and wrong, and our longing for justice, for love, for a better home.

The competition between religion and art for the territory of the human imagination has created longstanding hostility where it should have revealed a fundamental sympathy.

Imagination, which we need to create or confront art, is also required for every act of faith. We need imagination both to believe in a world beyond our own and envision a better hope for this one.

So art can be seen not as hostile to faith, but as practice for it. Building the muscle of imagination makes us better fit to believe. And love, the central command of faith, requires enormous imagination, to understand the life, feelings, or needs of someone else.

Faith and art are not enemies but sisters, both straining past the limits of this world to something greater. Each has something to teach the other.

Faith needs people who are experts in imagination to bear the burden of imagining, and to teach others how to do the work of imagination themselves.

Art can offer faith new ways to see, move, and speak.

And faith can offer art a history of thought, revelation, and practice to seek and understand the encounter with God that art knows by touch, if not by name.

ART AND WORSHIP

Despite the history of friction between art and religion, artists and audiences know that art can create a "religious experience"—the sensation that we're in the presence of something transcendent or divine.

In the TV show *Freaks and Geeks*, a teenager ends a conversation about God by declaring: "I believe in God, man. I've seen him. I've felt his power. He plays drums for Led Zeppelin and his name is John Bonham!"

Whether we're Zeppelin fans or not, all of us have had some variation of this experience: in a piece of art, we've had a glimpse of God.

Our responses to art can easily be taken for religious fervor. We are struck dumb before great paintings, shriek and shake at rock concerts, fork over huge amounts of cash to get a look at our favorite actor.

We preserve art objects like holy relics. We measure our days and weeks counting down to the next record release. We wear gear that signals that we're true believers. We look to art for meaning and healing. We build community around the art we love best. We evangelize our friends.

The spiritual power of art is so great that people around the world choose art over their real material needs: Cuban music lovers who walked for hours to attend all-night dance parties, American teenagers who skip lunch so they can spend their lunch money on music, secret librarians who risked their lives to preserve collections of banned books as Russian cities burned.

People who are suffering also reach for art, not just as a distraction, but as a weapon against pain. The abused child experiences the sight of something beautiful as a form of rescue. The bereaved mother finds comfort she can't explain in the lines of an abstract painting. The social worker begins to take photographs of any beauty she can find as an act of war against the evil that consumes the sex offenders with whom she spends her days.

Art has incredible powers, and many of them religion also claims: to illuminate, transform, heal, reveal, lead us into ecstasies, and bring us back to ourselves. And in recent years, as many cultures grow more secular, art has begun to step into religion's traditional role: to explain the world and help us negotiate with whatever mysteries lie beyond.

More and more of us no longer have regular religious practices. But we're still hungry for meaning, transcendence, and ritual. And many of us now turn to art to meet those needs.

Sometimes the substitution of art for religion is bizarrely precise. The Sunday morning service is replaced by the Sunday film series or concert. Art museums and libraries are pressed into service as a new kind of holy ground for the celebration of weddings.

Both art and religion also involve rituals that give the initiated a sense of belonging and self-righteousness, but provoke anxiety among newcomers—like the custom of not clapping between movements at classical concerts.

And we debate about art, from the merits of our favorite country stars, to the finer points of academic theory, with a passion and intolerance usually reserved for religion—because at root, conversations about both art and religion are conversations about God.

Our impulse to worship in the presence of art can lead us to treat artists as gods.

Artists are often seen, by both themselves and others, as an order of itinerants devoted to a mystery that they pursue with discipline and sacrifice that strongly echoes religious devotion. We discuss art and artists in tones of reverence and ecstasy usually reserved for the holy.

We even collect the relics of artists as if they were saints: the New York Public Library, for instance, recently put the bones of a Romantic poet on display, despite the fact that those bones can't be expected to offer insight into the poems the dead man left behind.

Some artists encourage this, to feed their egos or libidos, or to protect their careers in a climate in which worship is a major form of currency.

But artists are aware, sometimes to a painful degree, of the difference between their work and what they have to offer personally—like the famous guitarist who greets women who flock to him after performances with the rueful warning that "I cannot do to you what my guitar can do."

And accepting worship is profoundly dangerous for an artist.

People who believe we're part divine may stop telling us the truth about our work, or the world, or ourselves. Or they may do work for us that we could learn or grow from doing. And all of this can reduce the friction we need to reveal and refine our art.

Praise is also deeply fickle. It's often the most worshipful fans who turn vicious at the first sign of change or growth—the fans covered in tattoos from your last album who are quickest to denounce the next one. If we become dependent on external worship, the results can be catastrophic when that praise turns to criticism—or simply silence.

But the most fundamental danger for an artist is the way worship can compromise the core of our ability to create. When we begin to think of ourselves as godlike, it destroys the humility necessary to listen to and follow the voice of inspiration.

When religious authorities see people react to art with worship, they're often quick to discount it.

There's no point in worshipping art, some claim, because it's only ever a copy or a shadow of this extraordinary world, which they see as the creative masterpiece of God.

In the strictest sense, they're right. No architect has ever made anything as remarkable and vital as the simple spirals of morning glory buds on the scrap heap outside a cathedral. And no fictional character is ever as varied, complex, and specific as any human being.

Art, in this sense, always misses the mark. But it is also, always, far more than the sum of its parts. And to ignore art's power to elicit worship, despite its humble elements, is a form of the old heresy of gnosticism: a contempt for the world that leaves us unable to believe that God could actually be present in the stuff of this earth.

Art provokes worship of surprising power from people who are not actively seeking to worship anything. In some cases, they're actually resisting it. What they experience in art does not feel like an echo or an imitation. It has the force of an actual encounter with God.

Some artists even build a kind of personal faith around the moments of transcendence they find in creation. Instead of believing that they themselves are gods, they treat their artistic practice with religious devotion.

And the people who raise their lighters in praise at concerts, or choose a library as holy ground on which to marry, aren't mistaken about where God can be found. They recognize the power and holiness of the encounters they have in art. They are responding to the real presence of God.

But whether we're artists or art lovers, our encounters with art can't bear the strain of serving as religion.

Even the art that moves us most does not answer our fundamental questions of justice and meaning, life and death—or our need for love.

If we ask art to bear the weight of religion, it will come to pieces in our hands, or break and fail when we need it most.

But when we recognize art as the home of an encounter with God, we find both new ways to reckon with the power in art, and new paths to God.

WHO IS THE MUSE?

The idea that art flows from beyond the artist is ancient.

And it's persistent, perhaps because it serves as an explanation for the widespread sensation that inspiration comes from something beyond us.

But the concept of an external muse offers artists something else as well: a way to dodge many of the unpleasant consequences of creation.

If we claim the work doesn't really come from us, we can't be blamed for its limitations or failures. On the flip side, we can't be blamed for showing off: we're just following the orders of some irresistible force. And we can't be held responsible for work that might shock family members, offend polite society, or anger governments.

The violence in an artist's work, the bodies and minds laid bare, the hard truths told about ourselves and those who love us, the blistering social critique: with the scapegoat of a muse, artists can claim we're not really sure how any of this appears in our work. We're just discovering it ourselves. It comes as just as much of a surprise to us as to anyone else. The artist only picks up the pen or brush. It's the muse who moves it.

An artist can also invoke a muse to demand freedom in their personal life. How can a person be expected to be polite, pay bills, turn work in on time, stay faithful in love, deal with the drudgery of child-rearing, when we are both the victim and the mouthpiece of an unpredictable creative force entirely beyond our control?

But this understanding of the muse can be deadly. Countless artists have taken refuge in the muse only to find that their pose of losing control in creation turned to reality in ways that threatened not only their art but their lives.

Perhaps even more tragic are artists who confuse their addictions or excesses with "the muse" itself. They begin to believe that their songs flow from drink, their visions only appear out of opium dreams, their stories can only be found when they erase themselves with pleasure or pain. In pursuit of art, they give themselves over to addictions and obsessions that ultimately destroy their ability to create.

A muse may strike us as a more comfortable figure than a god.

We might shy away from the spiritual realm because we're afraid of what we'll discover there, because we've been abused by religious authority, or because we don't want to face the claims a god might make on us.

And why would an artist like Picasso, with a highly developed concept of a creative spirit, and a lifetime of successful negotiation with it, need to appeal to a god rather than a muse?

But taking refuge in the idea of a muse may simply trade one collection of powerful anxieties for another.

The instant we accept the existence of a muse, we must either wade into or ignore a host of profound questions about the nature and boundaries of the spiritual realm where the muse operates.

Are we a tool of inspiration, a child, a partner, a friend?

Does inspiration care for us, or is it willing to destroy us in pursuit of its own ends?

And what about the messages it transmits? These shapes, melodies, images, gestures: what are they for? Are they meant to shed light or deceive us, to distract us from the truth or point us to it, to lead us astray or bring us home?

Over years of work, we may become familiar with inspiration—or even expert in our negotiations with it.
But history is not a promise.
Even the most disciplined artists in the world are still subject to inspiration's fits: ideas that arrive, unbidden but insistent, even when an artist is outside the studio or away from the desk.
And the unpredictable intrusions of inspiration are a minor annoyance compared to the almost unnamable terror that, since we have no control of inspiration, no contract with it, it might abandon us without warning or explanation at any time.
This fear is amplified by the sense that we do not act alone in creation, and by the alienation we feel when we return to our best work.
We can't believe we made that.
So how can we know if we'll ever be able to again?

To name God as the source of inspiration provides a double-edged solution.
The artist loses the pride of absolute authorship. But most artists hold that pride with distinct unease, because of the strength of the sensation that something beyond us works through us in creation.
And as artists lose the illusion of absolute authorship, we gain the power of God.

The act of surrender has radically different meaning, depending on whether the force we surrender to can be trusted or not. If we surrender to a force we don't know or understand, out of weakness, greed, or self-preservation, surrender can be an act of cowardice, or even madness.

But surrender in trust can be an act of freedom and hope: a child who allows a parent to cover his eyes in preparation for a gift, one lover completely given over to another.

To locate the source of inspiration in God offers a vast tradition of wisdom, story, and practical tools to approach the spiritual realm that is inspiration's home.

We no longer operate based on guesswork about the moods of an unpredictable, unknowable muse.

Instead, creation is rooted in the history and promises of a living God, an endless source of inspiration, power, and love.

In creation, we have the sense that we touch something infinite. But our own energy, intelligence, skill, experience, honesty, all have painfully clear limits. If we are the only source of our art, we must one day run out. It's only a question of when.

Artists who believe we spend only from our own resources are always working against the day we will run out. We can never be sure when that day will come. Or be sure we'll recognize it when it does.

Some artists face this anxiety with a kind of tragic heroism, reveling in the fact that we may be completely consumed by the act of creation—like Edna St. Vincent Millay with her candle that burns at both ends.

But artists who see our art as the product of our own limited resources may also begin to hoard: not use our best ideas for fear they may also be our last, fail to put everything we have into every piece, for fear we'll be left with nothing.

Or we may mine ourselves frantically, trying to get out everything we can since we can't be sure we'll ever see it again—which results in lower quality work.

But the instant we recognize that inspiration comes from God, creation is no longer the consumption of our own diminishing resources.

Instead, it flows from the inexhaustible creative power of God, which can never run out, because it comes from something infinite.

As a result, we become both more humble, and more ambitious. Instead of thinking "I'm not that good," we can have both the courage and the humility to believe that something better than us could come through us.

Creation no longer seems like a fundamentally selfish act, nothing more than a way to indulge our own impulses. Instead, we create out of responsibility for a gift that's been put into our hands.

We no longer need to wear ourselves out, working against inspiration's unknown expiration date. Instead, we can take breaks from our work and build the strength to return to it fresh, certain that inspiration will still be there when we do.

Editing is no longer a process of self-amputation. Instead, we hunt through our work for signs of God: separating rock from gold, and forming raw gold into rings or foil.

This same faith allows us to discard anything we know to be second-rate, with the certainty that something better will come if we refuse to settle, and wait: not because we know we "have it in us," but because we believe we draw on something beyond ourselves.

Faith that art flows from God also eases our fear of exposure. To share our art is no longer a kind of psychic striptease. Our art is not fully ours. It never was. We are neither its true author, nor its true subject. Although we are sometimes illuminated by our art, it always reveals far more than us. And the more it surpasses us, the more powerful it becomes.

At the same time, we are protected from the trap of pride. We can't claim credit for our talent, or the inspiration we receive. Our accomplishment lies in stepping aside to let it through, and the service we devote to it. So we are less likely to fall victim to an inflated or easily wounded ego, which can mar or twist our art.

The belief that art flows from God can also balance and heal our relationships with other artists. We no longer compete for the attentions of a hazy and fickle muse. And there is no single prize we all seek. The question is no longer who has done it the best, but what traces of God's presence we can glimpse in the work of all artists.

Recognizing that inspiration flows from God both answers and annihilates the question of art's purpose.

Through history, all definitions of art have failed. They fail in the same way theology is frustrated by the beatific vision of a living God, and in the same way academic classifications fail to capture or express the riot of creation.

This is because art is of a piece with both God and creation, which are inexpressible as anything other than themselves.

To ask, "What is art for?" is just as absurd as asking, "What is a child for?" Or even, "What is God for?"

We can count up a child's activities and catalog their characteristics without ever coming close to understanding their purpose. In fact, any attempt to reduce a person to any one purpose—to earn money or prestige, to give another person pleasure, or even to "do good"—results in absurdity, or obscenity.

Like God, and the whole of creation, art constantly escapes our clumsy attempts to define and use it for our own ends.

Art offers us countless gifts, but it can never be defined by any—or all—of them.

Because inspiration comes from God, we can't earn or command it.

But it is always present and always speaking.

Our experience of inspiration is not uncertain and unreliable because inspiration is, but because we are.

What seem to be episodes of inspiration are those rare points when our own voice goes still and our defenses drop, so we can hear the voice of inspiration.

Often, these moments occur when we think we aren't doing much at all: early in the morning, when our hands are soapy with dishwater—or on the steering wheel of a car.

"It doesn't care what you are doing when it comes together," says songwriter Tom Waits. ". . . Often it finds you when you don't want to work. You're driving along and you have to pull over and put your sandwich in your lap and get out a piece of paper, and you have to write a thing. But there's the thousand times when you've sat there with the same empty piece of paper in a house with the window open and the birds are singing and . . . nothing. . . .

"It's not about making a fist; it's about opening your hand."

Some encounters with God transfigure and heal us. Some lay us bare.

When our plans come to pieces in the hands of God, we may feel free, or lost. When our masks and defenses burn away in the presence of God, we may feel fully revealed, or totally naked. Or we may feel all of them, in the same moment.

The transforming power of an encounter with God is the root of many of the contradictions in our reactions to art. It is what draws us to art, and why we fear it. It is why we both long to create, and avoid it.

We rarely clear space in our lives for an encounter with inspiration. Even when we have established consistent artistic disciplines, we often pick up a brush, confront a blank page, hold the instrument ready in our hands with an air of command, our minds still ringing with noise that we have never developed the mental muscle to still.

Perhaps loudest of all may be the sound of our own demands: when we cry so loudly for inspiration that we can't hear anything it's already saying, when we insist we must be this kind of artist and not that, when we attempt to force a piece in our own preconceived direction, rather than waiting for inspiration to reveal it whole, uncompromised, and often a complete surprise.

But the blocks we hit in those moments are not punishment, but revelation, if we have the eyes to see it.

They teach us that inspiration is not given to us to advance our own interests, or even to give our lives meaning.

It may bless, change, and shape us, but it is not ours.
It will not obey us because it was never our property.
It's given to us as a gift to the world.

The most important consequence of recognizing that art flows from God is not in our art, but our lives.

Some people, and some artists, think that an artist's life hardly matters—only our art. So artists can, or even should, allow other areas of our life to wither, as long as our art flourishes.

Some even think that art is so valuable that it makes anything we suffer, or any suffering we inflict, irrelevant.

Or that our art can erase or redeem our personal failings, like the musician whose flaws we want to forget as soon as he opens his mouth to sing.

But art does not force us, or allow us, to shed the contradictions and frustrations of our own lives. The world is littered with artists whose undeniable accomplishments are permanently tainted by their faults, from Ezra Pound's and Richard Wagner's support of fascism, to Harvey Weinstein's and Bill Cosby's abuse of women.

All of them produced work of transcendent quality.

And all of their work is thrown into question by their lives.

The circumstances of our lives affect everything about our art: the clarity of our vision, the precision of our technique—even how much art we are able to create.

Our financial struggles can force us to produce according to the whims of the market, rather than the voice of inspiration. Our relationships can create so much noise and stress that we cease to create at all.

So artists need a God for the same reason any of us do: to heal, guide, and anchor us, not just in our art, but in our life.

Connection with God can keep us from being caught in a constant chase after sensation and validation that can blunt our ability to hear the voice of inspiration, or sap our courage to respond to it.

It offers comfort in seasons when what we need most is simply to wait and rest.

It provides us with a broader cosmology and a moral vision that can shield us from excess and protect us from the lie that our only value lies in what we are able to create.

It frees our art from the pressure it bears when it is the central source of comfort and meaning in our lives. Instead, art comes from the source of all comfort and meaning.

And as our connection with God releases the pressure our art once bore, we gain new freedom as we create.

ART AND LOVE

The foundational element in an artist's relationship with God is love.
    A muse may provoke, torment, tease, or reward us.
    But it doesn't love us, or encourage us to love, as God does.
    And love is the antidote for the greatest enemy of art—fear.
    The primary obstacle to creation is fear: of facing ourselves, God, others, the unknown, exposure, vulnerability, failure, success.
    It's fear, not laziness, that paralyzes us as artists.
    Strength is no match for fear. No matter how strong we are, we are always susceptible to a stronger fear. And one of fear's powers is its ability to endlessly expand.
    Hope is no match for fear, either. Our hopes are often woefully misplaced. And they are constantly betrayed.
    But love casts out fear. No terror is as terrible if we know we are loved. In fact, our terror of being unloved is so great that we are willing to endure all kinds of terrors simply for the illusion of love, or one of its substitutes: power, ambition, greed, lust.
    Love cancels our deepest fear and shrinks all others.
    It gives us both strength and hope.
    And it puts us in the strongest position to create.

Anxiety and ambition are both powerful masters, but cruel. The only prize ambition offers is a world that is notoriously fickle. The only thing we can win from anxiety is its absence. And both anxiety and ambition are, at root, symptoms of our need for love.

But when we work out of that need, no matter what we create, we will always fail, because we can't earn love.

We can recognize and nurture love, or reject and destroy it. But we can't create love by our own actions.

Like inspiration itself, we can only welcome love by surrender. Love is a species of grace: the delight a lover takes in who we are, regardless of anything we do.

For an artist to create out of love may be one of the most vulnerable acts of love in the world. It involves all the risk of any love—but it is also directed into the complete unknown.

Artists who create out of love don't have the luxury of choosing our lovers, of watching for their response, of explaining or defending ourselves. And acts of love are far harder to explain, both to ourselves and others, than acts of ambition or anxiety.

Leaning on the love of God allows us to love with the recklessness that art requires: with our whole selves, with total vulnerability, and with complete uncertainty about whether or not our love will be returned.

Because God lives beyond time, God's love is not threatened by the same things that threaten other kinds of love: change, chance, and death.

All love is a reflection of God's love, but unrooted in God, it can quickly burn to ash, harden to obsession, or fade into habit.

But the love of God reorganizes our hearts so that our love becomes more like God's, unchanging and endless. It nourishes us, so that we don't always have to demand love in exchange for the love we give. And it protects us, so that we can afford to take the risk of loving—not because we trust the response of others, but because we are transformed and sustained by the love of God.

Love is the most powerful motive for creation in the world. Unlike anxiety and ambition, which ultimately paralyze or burn us out, love renews and sustains both itself and us.

It is constantly active: one of the clearest traits of love is the sense that we could never do enough to express it.

And it is endlessly creative, both in the variety of its expressions, and in how far it will go to overcome any challenge it meets.

We create because we love.

And we create because we are loved.

BOOK TWO
INCARNATION

Inspiration, the presence of God that sparks all art, comes with a sense of infinite possibility. In its grip, artists have the sense that we can both make and break worlds.

But in the end, all we have to build with is this one: the words and songs of our mother's tongue, the stones and pigments of this earth.

This is the miracle of incarnation—the immortal spirit of inspiration both revealed and bound by the finite elements of this world.

Among all miracles, incarnation may be the deepest mystery. On the surface, it doesn't interrupt nature's known laws—change water to wine, split the sea. Incarnation doesn't even meet an immediate need: feed us or heal us or sweep away an enemy.

But by clothing the infinite in the finite, incarnation makes the finite infinite.

A god revealed in ordinary matter also reveals the underlying glory of all matter, no matter how humble.

At the same time, the presence of a transcendent and eternal God reveals the total inadequacy of any matter to express God.

Without seeming to disturb a thing, the miracle of incarnation both transfigures the whole world, and threatens its foundations.

It doesn't suspend any single law.

It upends all of them.

THE MECHANICS OF INCARNATION

Artists have been trying to describe the mechanics of incarnation—the interplay between the inbreaking of inspiration and their own thoughts, talent, heart, and life—for as long as they've been making art.

"A man's life is interwoven into his music," says jazz legend Dizzie Gillespie. "You can't help it from coming out."

In order to create, says poet Marie Howe, "you have to be there and you have to disappear . . . writing is pretty much a relief from the self—and yet the self has to be utterly there."

But artists offer a wide variety of descriptions of how that process works.

"I never thought of myself as being what they call a genius," says dancer and choreographer Martha Graham. "I don't know what genius is. I think a far better expression is a retriever, a lovely strong golden retriever that brings things back from the past, or retrieves things from our common blood memory."

Poet Ralph Waldo Emerson uses a similar metaphor, but in his version, the artist is not an animal, but the animal's rider: "the poet knows that he speaks adequately then only when he speaks somewhat wildly, or 'with the flower of the mind,' not with the intellect used as an organ, but with the intellect released from all service and suffered to take its direction from its celestial life. . . . As the traveler who has lost his way throws his reins on his horse's neck and trusts to the instinct of the animal to find his road, so must we do with the divine animal who carries us through this world."

Artists as diverse as Questlove, David Byrne, Katharine Anne Porter, Stephen King, and Ernest Hemingway have all compared artists to wells that fill slowly with the water of inspiration. As Hemingway puts it: "There are as many kinds of wells as there are writers. The important thing is to have good water in the well, and it is better to take a regular amount out than to pump the well dry and wait for it to refill."

Some artists, like Paul Simon, experience themselves as transmitters: radio operators or perhaps even radio receivers, that pick up distant stations others might only hear as static.

This metaphor makes the absurdity of looking for the source of art in the artist especially clear: it would be like taking apart a radio and expecting to find a symphonic orchestra inside.

Artists also have something in common with miners. Miners don't put gold in the ground. Until they take it out, it's there for anyone with the right equipment to find. Strength, skill, and stubbornness are required to dig shafts, strike ore, then carry it back up to the surface. Developing that strength and skill can take years.

Without them, a miner can't mine. But without ore, a miner's skills are useless.

But the comparison with mining for ore, which waits patiently in place, sometimes for eons, doesn't capture the dynamic force of inspiration, which many artists experience as a power that pushes them in directions they didn't expect to go.

So artists may be even more like engineers and roughnecks who drill for oil or water, which have an energy and trajectory of their own. Sometimes it takes enormous ingenuity and effort to locate water and pump it up from hidden caves. But sometimes, once oil is struck, it bursts forth with such force that all you can do is get out of the way.

The artist's sensation that art has a life of its own can also be expressed in the metaphor of artist as cultivator: gardener or farmer.

The patterns of the farmer's life do bear some resemblance to the artist's. Both require preparation: of a field, of a canvas, of the artist themselves. The care and skill in that preparation have a great deal to do with what the farmer or the artist will be able to produce. Both the artist and the farmer shepherd a mysterious process largely beyond their control: at some points, there is nothing for either of them to do but wait for something to grow.

Even when the seed is beyond their reach—below ground, or deep under the surface of their thoughts—both the farmer and the artist must still be vigilant to nurture and defend it. Both must also be wise about the time to harvest—not too early or too late. And both must then sort and prepare whatever was gathered in the fever of harvest.

Both the artist and the farmer also devote all this care and sacrifice in the service of something that they can only care for, never command.

If a farmer never plants a seed, no crop will ever grow—just as, if an artist never picks up a pen, they will never sketch an image or record a poem.

But no farmer can make their own seed from scratch, or give life to a seed that has died. And without a living seed, either of grain or inspiration, all the work an artist or a farmer can do will produce nothing but dust.

Still, the farmer's work is radically different from the artist's in one key respect: the farmer does not plant seed in their own flesh, and the seed does not produce a crop from elements of the farmer's own life or mind. A farmer's character may affect a crop, but no farmer's crop ever captures and reveals their character in the way art both captures and reveals an artist's.

So the most perfect metaphor for an artist in creation is a woman who gives birth.

Pregnancy, childbirth, and motherhood all demand courage and strength. But a woman does not contain in herself all the elements necessary for conception. Like inspiration, the seed of creation must come from another source. That connection is deeply embedded in many languages, which use the same words—conceive, concept, conception—to describe the advent of both a child and a thought.

Both before and after conception, a woman's choices shape her child, just as an artist's choices shape their work. Some of the choices are incremental, like what she eats or drinks each day. Some of them are profound, like the identity of the father. Some of them may require great effort, to break addictions or create a home.

But an enormous amount of the process is beyond the woman's control, or even reach. She does not consciously dictate the division of cells, the architecture of organs, her child's sex or hair color, or even the moment of birth.

At the same time, every child is fully clothed in a mother's flesh. In the womb, a child's entire body and mind are soaked in whatever flows through the mother: the chemical traces of wine or sugar, fear or joy, dissolved in blood. The child hears what the mother hears, moves when she moves, shakes when she laughs. And to a great extent, parents continue to create an equally all-consuming climate for their children even after birth.

But the qualities a woman has the least control over are the ones that will likely affect her child the most: not the surface decisions of readying a nursery or researching childhood development, but the tragedies and strengths that lie in wait in both the woman's ancestral genetic codes and her own character, the sum of the choices she's made in response to the events that shaped her life.

Not only that, but the great pressures that shape our lives—and our children, and our art—are almost always ones we do not choose, and cannot control: love, loss, injustice, war, beauty, talent, luck, hardship. Even things we've long forgotten affect both our children and our art.

And we are shaped most deeply by exactly those things we are least able to choose.

Maddeningly, and sometimes heartbreakingly, both our children and our art are shaped far less by what we want to say than by who we are. Our children don't learn by choice and analysis. They learn by mimicry, from example. The characteristics that will emerge most surely in our children—or our art—will be the ones that we embody most deeply ourselves.

Our children, and our art, inexorably reveal us, preserving and amplifying our beauty and our flaws, our deepest desires and beliefs, whether we've admitted them to ourselves or not.

Our art, like our children, may transcend and resist us in ways that both dazzle and baffle us. But no politics or point of view can ever be successfully inserted in our art by conscious thought at the moment of creation. That kind of calculation, in that crucial moment, will only result in failure.

If we wish anything to appear in our art—wisdom, courage, compassion, justice, fire—we must first allow it to shape our own being so completely that it can't fail to emerge in what we create.

Both a child and our art take in everything, use everything, and are affected by everything we do. This makes the projects of parenting and art both infinite and endless, invading and requiring our whole life, and revealing even parts of ourselves we've forgotten, hidden, or never knew existed.

But at the same time, nothing is too small or insignificant, too broken, dark, or bent for inspiration to use. Failure, pain, sorrow—even experiences the artist counted a meaningless waste—are all transfigured by inspiration into art.

As artists, we may be overwhelmed by the realization of how deeply all aspects of our lives inflect our art—and how deeply we must change to see any change in our art, or lives.

But in that same moment, our whole life can be transformed by the realization that every moment of any day, no matter how unexpected or unlikely, can feed and shape our art.

The parent and the artist both bear enormous responsibility, even long after we may long to give it up. Our smallest choices can have unimaginable repercussions in the life of our child, or our art. They can determine whether the child or the art ever exists at all, and whether they survive in life.

But despite the resemblance any child bears to her parents, no child is simply an extension of their family. Even in the womb, where all nutrients originally flow into a baby's system through the mother's blood, a child's blood type may be distinct. Both art and children are meant to take on a life of their own, independent of the mother or the artist.

And thriving children, or true art, are not created through strict conscious control.

The more we try to control our art, or a child, the more likely we are to lose all control, and destroy what we sought to nurture.

We succeed, as artists or as parents, not by our attempts at control, but by the choices we make about who we are, as we prepare ourselves to be the home for the accomplishment of a mystery.

THE UNIVERSAL VOICE

The instant we begin to suspect that inspiration flows from a spirit beyond us, a question arises.

If all art flows from a single source, why is it not uniform?
Why don't all poems break forth in the tongue of angels?
Why don't all singers sing the same song?
Why don't all dancers turn together in one universal dance?

Many artists have observed a surprising, indefinable unity in art that persists through history, across genres, and in artists of radically different backgrounds.

Borges collects a number of these observations in the opening paragraph of his essay "Coleridge's Flower":

> Around 1938, Paul Valery wrote: "the history of literature should not be the history of authors and the course of their careers or the career of their works, but rather the history of the Spirit as the producer or consumer of literature; such history could be written without mentioning a single writer." It was not the first time the Spirit had made this observation; in 1844, one of its amanuenses in Concord had noted: "I am very much struck in literature by

the appearance that one person wrote all the books." . . . Twenty years earlier, Shelley expressed the opinion that all the poems of the past, present, and future were episodes or fragments of a single infinite poem, written by all the poets on earth.

In other writings, Borges claims that this Spirit is not just the author of all art, but author of the entire world: "We (the indivisible divinity that works in us) have dreamed the world. We have dreamed it resistant, mysterious, visible, ubiquitous in space and firm in time, but we have allowed slight, and eternal, bits of the irrational to form part of its architecture so as to know that it is false."

The idea that the world itself is the creation of a powerful spirit is not new. It lies at the root of the Hebrew creation story, as well as the creation stories of many other traditions.

But Borges is not just interested in a spirit who created the world. He's suggesting that creatures of this world participate in an ongoing act of creation, in partnership with that spirit. And when Borges conflates creature and creator—"we (the indivisible divinity that works in us)"—he points to how difficult it is to distinguish between creature and creator in the moment a creature creates.

At the moment of creation, inspiration and the artist intermingle and fuse. For artists, this involves both great loss and great gain. Our identity is consumed, but at the same time, something divine has come alive inside us. Our movements are no longer our own, but we are no longer bound by the limits of this world: the inrushing god sets us free from its physics and fears.

Ironically, it's often in the midst of that fusion that we meet ourselves most fully. "I never completely forget myself except when I am writing," Flannery O'Connor says. "And I am never more completely myself than when I am writing."

But despite the sense that our best work emerges when we most fully forget ourselves, clear signs of the individual artist remain in every work of art. We know at once whether we are listening to Ella

Fitzgerald or Bach, looking at Picasso or Rembrandt, reading Hawthorne or Zora Neale Hurston. Borges himself is instantly recognizable, often from a single sentence of a minor work.

Even artists in the same tradition, at the same moment in history—like Mavis Staples and Aretha Franklin—are easy to distinguish from each other. In fact, these two singers present an interesting test case for the role of incarnation in art. Neither is known primarily as a writer. But both are capable of producing a new work of art simply by incarnating a song within herself: the unique way music echoes through her body and soul. Their recordings of "Amazing Grace" are not just minor variations on a well-known theme. They are distinct and necessary works of art.

Art offers evidence of a universal, in-breaking creative force. But it is also inflected by whatever it flows through, like water flavored by the taste of the stones it rushes over, pink salt or yellow diamonds.

Art is sparked by inspiration that transcends this world and leads us far beyond ourselves.

But it is also fully, stubbornly incarnate.

INCARNATION AND AUDIENCE

Art is not born when inspiration speaks into the cold dark of space, but when inspiration echoes in a human mind and heart.

And no matter what genre an artist works in, the human heart and mind are every artist's final medium.

At first glance, an audience may not seem to have much to do with the process of creation.

Sometimes artists refine our work in reaction to an audience: a comedian drops a joke that never lands, a director cuts a scene where the crowd always gets restless.

The appetites of an audience may also influence the kind of art an artist makes. Fabergé could not have executed his visions with precious metal and gems if his pieces were not in vogue with the Russian aristocracy. The novella thrives in modern Japan, where it is considered an important literary form, but is essentially unsaleable in the United States, where the book-buying audience won't fork over a price high enough to make slight volumes pay.

Still, no audience, according to the traditional view, fundamentally alters a work of art. We may weep or spit at the sight of a canvas, but that does not change its colors. We may leave a play baffled, angry, or half-asleep, but we do not rewrite the script.

But the reality of the relationship between art and audience is far more complex. If art has any intrinsic value apart from an audience, no human being is capable of knowing it. Our only means for perceiving art is the human mind and heart.

For some art forms, like poems or novels, this is painfully clear. What is the point of a book, without a human imagination to transform ink on paper into images and thought?

Highly embodied art forms like dance, architecture, and sculpture may seem to have some substance or even life of their own. But they don't succeed or fail simply by the bare fact of their existence. Their meaning or worth is only revealed in their power to move a person.

Inspiration is not fully incarnate in the moment that we pin it to a page or capture it in clay, but in its ultimate act: when it comes to life again within someone else. A painting is not completed when the oil and pigment finish drying on canvas, but every time a new pair of eyes takes it in.

Because all of us have different desires and defenses, every person who looks at a canvas sees a different painting. Any book is actually many books—as many books as the number of its readers, who all furnish each character with a different face, who all imagine every scene in a different place.

A single play has as many versions as the number of patrons in a theater. A woman may leave a movie with the uneasy feeling that she has just seen a tragedy, while her husband enjoyed himself thoroughly.

We do not simply respond to some external thing called "art." In the moment we confront a piece, we are the actual location of that art, as the spirit that inspired it becomes incarnate again, in us.

So every piece of art is created, in part, by the character of each member of its audience—the same way that every piece of art is formed, in part, by the character of each artist.

This doesn't mean that the tastes of any given audience determine the fundamental value of a piece of art. Happily drunk, bar patrons will clap for almost anything on stage. Cowed by an artist's prestige, audience members, including critics, may spill volumes of praise on a mediocre piece.

Some of the qualities of genuine art—the ache beauty provokes, the questions art refuses to answer, the demands it makes, the vertigo of unfamiliarity—may make art less popular than the comforts we find in pornography, propaganda, and entertainment.

But no audience member is ever truly passive in an encounter with art.

And the resistance of some audiences can't erase the presence of inspiration that sparks and defines art, or the unique power of that art to inhabit and move us.

THE CASCADE OF INCARNATION

Even the greatest performer is also a member of the audience.

In order to sing, she must be the first to listen to a song.

Artists seem to fall into two broad categories: performers and composers.

Composers are the songwriters, the choreographers, the authors, directors, painters, sculptors, architects. They draw the plan, set the score, write the script that a performer follows. Or they create artifacts like novels, paintings, or sculptures, which seem to require no performer.

Performers are the actors, musicians, dancers, designers, camera crews, translators. They bring their spirit and skill to bear in the service of another artist's vision.

Some artists—the conductor, the performance artist, the singer-songwriter, the comedian who writes her own jokes, the producer who shapes an album, the DJ who blends songs he didn't write, the director who casts himself as star—clearly straddle this line.

But the deeper reality is that all artists create by a process of incarnation, and every piece of art requires performers. Some performances are just more public than others.

It's clear that a director can't mount a play without a cast and crew. But novelists, painters, and architects all have performers, too: everyone who reads their book or looks at their painting. And all the people who live in, or pass by, a building they conceived.

The director of a play has the advantage of working directly with his performers. Those relationships may be complex and even fraught. But when confusion or conflict arises, the actor can ask questions and the director can answer—and vice versa. Both actors and directors also have the advantage of immediate reaction from a live audience.

But novelists, painters, and architects are rarely present to direct the performance of their work, or to see how it is received.

Not only that, but a director's performers are generally artists who have devoted significant preparation to build the skills they need to bring the vision of another artist to life.

Novels, paintings, and buildings, on the other hand, are mainly performed by amateurs: the casual reader, the weekend art-goer, the stray glance of the person on the street.

But at the deepest level, there is no such thing as performer or audience: only inspiration that cascades through a vast variety of hearts and minds.

Inspiration first comes directly, to the original composer. It is refracted and amplified by dancers, actors, musicians, builders. And it is finally complete as it lights in each viewer's mind: when a delivery man leaves a store whistling a tune he just heard there on the radio, when the crowd at a concert begins to sing along.

In some genres, this cascade of inspiration is recognized and even encouraged. Much jazz, for instance, is based on performers reinhabiting the compositions of others. In other genres, the debts one artist owes another may be considered shameful, and deliberately obscured.

But no composer is a god who simply dictates an inflexible vision to passive performers. Without strong performers, the composer's original vision is marred, or comes to nothing. And the more deeply a performer welcomes a composer's original vision, the more completely the performer's own spirit transforms that vision.

In the same way, performers are not all-powerful magicians who cast spells on a defenseless audience. Each member of the audience comes to a piece with thoughts, fears, and desires so powerful that they all create their own unique work of art.

At every stage of creation—composer, performer, audience—inspiration becomes incarnate.

At any stage, the composer, performer, or audience may welcome inspiration or resist it.

At every stage, each participant is a kind of conductor, both moved by the music, and moving it.

And at every stage inspiration is most fully realized when it most fully inhabits a human being: the composer both lost and found in their vision, the performer both transfigured and revealed in performance, the audience members translated to a new world, creating new worlds of our own, and made new ourselves.

INCARNATION AND DIFFICULTY

Some artists seem to have almost perfect freedom in their response to inspiration. Paint, words, and notes all seem to offer limitless possibility. Nothing stops a songwriter from choosing the next chord.

Other artists, like film directors, orchestral composers, and architects, need vast quantities of money, materials, and fellow artists to create at all. Their challenges in making inspiration incarnate are obvious, and inescapable. "You dream wonderful things," says architect Jeremy Edmiston. "But then there's gravity."

But no inspiration ever becomes incarnate as art without some difficulty: the limits of language, the constraints of canvas and paint, the tolerances of wood and glass, and even the bounds of perception itself.

The difficulty of incarnation could be seen as nothing but a series of obstacles that stand between the artist and the achievement of some glowing image we receive from beyond. And some artists do see difficulty as a threat to our art. We can't paint, we believe, without the perfect pigment, play through anything but a perfectly balanced sound system, write in anything but a perfectly clean and quiet room, with half a dozen sharpened pencils, all pointed west.

This fight to find a perfect material, the refusal to settle for the second-rate, the careful nurture of our own best rhythms and practices, can be a way to honor inspiration, evidence of our desire to incarnate it in a pure and lasting form.

But we may also use any hint of difficulty as an excuse to avoid the demands of inspiration. How can we be expected to write, draw, sing, think, if someone keeps shouting outside, if the light is not perfect?

We can also hide in these questions from the much deeper challenge of creation itself. It's easier to confront the simple problems of the material world than to come defenseless to an encounter with inspiration.

But an artist who refuses to create under difficult conditions can veer quickly into artistic paralysis, since the conditions for creation are almost never perfect. And when our insistence on perfection prevents us from creating, we've betrayed inspiration in the most fundamental way, because no trace of it, however imperfect, can ever enter the world through us. Our insistence on the "perfect" expression of inspiration can actually result in its annihilation.

For some artists, this may even come as a relief. We have so many fears about making art that we would rather avoid it. And the fiction that we can't create unless the conditions are perfect is a perfect excuse. We seem very concerned about our art. So concerned that we never have to make it.

But inspiration is not a delicate element, vulnerable to any hint of difficulty. It can withstand all kinds of mistreatment. Somehow, much of the power of Shakespeare still survives in German translations stripped of his signature language and supplied with alternate endings that translators believed improved on the original. Masterworks of painting are plastered on t-shirts, tote bags, and umbrellas, because even reproduced as poorly color-balanced silkscreens, they still retain a large measure of their beauty and power. Musicians sweat for days to get the perfect sound on tape, but the energy of an inspired performance still pulses through the static of distant stations picked up on cheap car radios.

It's clear that too much constraint, especially in the form of poverty and stress, can crush an artist. And the removal of those difficulties can lead to profound flowering of important work. When patrons made it possible for Zora Neale Hurston to devote her time exclusively to writing, she produced her most substantial books.

But the removal of all difficulty frequently results in worse work, not better. Many artists, freed from constraint, begin to flounder, undone by ease and comfort: the fierce film star who descends into caricatures of his early performances, the incendiary pop singer defanged by fame, the writer so well respected no one dares edit him, who has therefore ceased to put out books that matter.

The history of art is also full of instances of difficulty that does not resist inspiration, but prompts it. The rich vocal harmonies of gospel music can be attributed in part to the fact that they were created by people without easy access to instruments. Milos Forman, director of *One Flew Over the Cuckoo's Nest*, was no doubt frustrated when, according to Hollywood rumor, both Marlon Brando and Gene Hackman turned down the starring role. But those refusals cleared the way for newcomer Jack Nicholson, who turned the opportunity into a signature role, and the film into a classic. The famous gold and turquoise constellations on the dome of Grand Central Station were only commissioned when Cornelius Vanderbilt discovered he didn't have enough money left to afford a glass ceiling. And Shaun Tan's frustration with his limited ability to influence story as a commercial illustrator inspired him to create his groundbreaking picture book, *The Arrival*.

Difficulty can even give birth to new artistic forms. Hemingway knew he had significant limits as a writer. So he invented a new minimalism that, for better or worse, shaped American letters for decades to come. Iggy Pop chafed at the limits of contemporary pop, which led him to lay the foundations of punk rock. The original sonnets and sonatas, ghazals and haiku, the demands of ballet and the conventions of blues were all born when artists voluntarily imposed limits on themselves. And those structures and limitations can play an important role in welcoming inspiration, calming our panic over the totally blank page or unmapped universe so that we can hear inspiration speak.

Today, technology has freed artists from much of the difficulty that marked an artist's life in the past: the actual physical challenges of carving stone, building believable monsters out of paper and gunpowder, struggling with the moody chemistry of photography, or writing out *War and Peace* in longhand. But contemporary artists continue to impose new constraints on themselves, sometimes more severe than either the market or convention demands.

As the film industry evolved to a point where it could effectively fake snow, or even sunlight, director Terrence Malick began to film only with natural light, in particular the "golden hours"—the first and last of the day—an incredible constraint for production crews that might otherwise work around the clock and long into the night, with the aid of artificial light. Jack and Meg White embarked on their remarkable exercise in stripping down the classic four-piece rock band to a drum kit and a single guitar just as an explosion in affordable digital capability had suddenly provided musicians with more possibilities than most of them could exploit in several lifetimes—a range so vast it could actually be paralyzing.

And all artists have experienced a moment when a mistaken note, a slip of the pen, an overheated piece of precious metal, or even a joke made at a point of frustration suddenly emerges as the heart of a whole piece. The tolerances of wood can dictate the curve of an architect's design—and its grain, which the architect can never fully control, may also provide the most striking element of an entire room.

In those moments, difficulty doesn't threaten inspiration. It welcomes it, derailing our tight control and conscious plans so that inspiration can break in. It may even be that in those moments, God breaks into the creative process in a different way, and speaks not just as inspiration, but through the elements of the created world: that listening to wood or stone, to light or sound, is another kind of revelation, of listening to God.

Difficulty doesn't weaken inspiration. It strengthens it, in the same way that creatures that struggle through birth gain strength for life. When we must fight to make inspiration incarnate, we discard everything unnecessary and keep only what is worth fighting for. This concentrates our art into its purest form, stripped of distractions and false gestures.

Difficulty reveals possibility. We may believe we've come to the end of our inspiration or ability, but if a final movement is required to complete a piece, or a corner of the building site is not yet complete, or a further thought is necessary to meet the formal standards of a poem, we may press on and discover even more inspiration than we'd dared hope.

Difficulty can also build the personal strength an artist needs to seek inspiration, and the courage to respond to it. Difficulty confronts us constantly with the humbling fact that we do not command everything we see—which is also the crucial dynamic in the process of creation. And difficulty forces us into areas beyond our control, which is exactly where we find inspiration.

Difficulty can become a crutch. It is easier to recognize, explain, and sell than inspiration. So some art markets prefer to judge and fund work based on its measurable difficulty, rather than the always immeasurable presence of inspiration.

Some artists may introduce excessive difficulty to our work to protect ourselves from our fears. If we embark on an extremely difficult project, we can always blame any disappointment on its difficulty, instead of ourselves.

But most artists do not need to seek additional difficulty.

The world provides more than enough of it for all lives, and all art.

And when we welcome difficulty, it can provide gifts we might never find if the world bent perfectly to our will: the way wood warps with time, the true story we discover amid the ruins of our prettiest lies.

Difficulty may take the shape of poetic form or client demands, the number of human fingers or the tolerances of gold or steel. But no matter where we find it, difficulty is not the enemy of inspiration, but a close companion.

INCARNATION IN CULTURE

Inspiration appears in a dizzying variety of times and places. It dictates in Homer's ancient Greek and through the keys of Lamont Dozier's piano. It catalogs the chickens, snow, eels, and chrysanthemums of Jakuchu's Colorful Realm. It breaks apart the English language in Emily Dickinson's hands. It births the tango on the floor of an Argentine bordello.

Inspiration's presence in the wide range of human cultures can be seen as God's celebration of every individual culture, and God's celebration of their huge variety: God's celebration of all cultures.

In every culture, art is both an alien voice, and that culture's highest achievement. Art contradicts a culture's conventional wisdom, threatens established authority, and even questions reality. At the same time, it captures a culture's inimitable habits and idiosyncrasies, smells, sights, sounds, anxieties, and dreams. But as art absorbs all these, it also transfigures them. Even a culture's most familiar elements, in the grasp of art, suddenly seem new and strange.

Inspiration's voice, and the art that it sparks, also threaten to erase the neat lines people often attempt to draw between cultures. Art has been used to strengthen national identity, create tribal loyalty, and mark class. But it also confuses national borders, tribal affiliations, and class distinctions.

Tango is unquestionably an expression of the barrios that birthed it. But it also carries some essence of those barrios across oceans that most of the children of those barrios will never cross, and into halls of wealth and power where they would not be welcome. We dance to the music of people we will never speak with, read intimate details of the lives of people we could never meet, stare into portraits of people we might look away from if we met them on the street.

It's voyeurism and theft to harvest a culture's art with no care for the people who created it. But art can also cross barriers the people who created it cannot, and break those barriers down. The political leaders of the American Civil Rights Movement of the 1960s were crucial to its success. But so were Black performers, from Sam Cooke to the Motown Revue, whose music was so powerful that audiences began to desegregate in order to hear it.

Art has a remarkable power to transcend culture: Michael Jackson, a kid from Gary, Indiana, can dominate pop charts in both Nigeria and Japan, and Jackie Chan's inimitable blend of Chinese opera training, martial arts, and charisma can dominate movie screens in Gary, Indiana.

Art also transcends time: centuries after their death, both Shakespeare's and Bach's works are performed around the world, and jokes of Greek comedy written before the time of Christ can still land with a twenty-first-century audience.

But even as art outlasts cultures, it also preserves them. Dante's *Commedia* is an extraordinary book regardless of a reader's grasp on thirteenth-century Florentine history. But Dante's observations on human nature and spectacular guesses about the geography of the spiritual realm are fully incarnate in the language and the culture in which Dante lived: the details of daily life, the political wrangling, the tawdry scandals, all trapped like bees in the enduring resin of his story. We cannot fully understand its timeless observations unless we understand Dante's own time and place.

No matter how thoroughly art transcends this world, it is also indelibly marked by whatever part of the world it is born into.

INCARNATION AND IMITATION

The clear mark of time and place on art can lead to an illusion: that art is only imitation, or recombination, of the elements of this world.

Imitation is one of the earliest explanations for art. Aristotle claimed that poetry springs from the human instinct to imitate what we see. But even as he makes this claim, the definition begins to escape him. Almost immediately, he admits that the act of imitation is also an act of transformation: "objects which in themselves we view with pain, we delight to contemplate when reproduced."

The idea of art as imitation persisted through the classical age, and later gained traction among religious thinkers, who dressed it up in the guise of humility. According to this religious twist, no artist could ever, or should ever, do more than imitate what God, the only Creator, has already made.

This view of art as imitation is convenient for religious authority. It places the bulk of God's creative activity safely in the distant past. It denies the troublesome possibility that a force as powerful and unpredictable as a god might intrude into the neat categories of present-day religious power and practice. It defines the artist's life as a mechanical experiment, and it denies the possibility of any genuine exchange between God and an artist—especially any exchange that might take place beyond the reach of religious authority.

But when this view of art appears within traditions that contain the Hebrew creation stories, it conflicts with another foundational doctrine: that humans are made in the image of God.

The belief that humans bear the image of God raises another tantalizing possibility: artists might be capable of more than imitation. They might share God's ability to create.

But for most of history, when either artists or religious thinkers arrived at this conclusion, they quickly defused it with caveat that our human creative impulse must only be a shadow or echo of God's creative force, not an active intrusion by God.

It's a dodge that releases both religious authority and artists from the fear—and the possibility—that an artist's work is, in fact, a constant negotiation with a living God.

Contemporary thinking recognizes that art has never been a process of simple imitation. Art doesn't just repeat the world. It imposes a point of view, if only in what it chooses to repeat.

So instead of talking about imitation, some now use a vocabulary of "recombination."

According to this view, the artist's fundamental act is to recycle materials and experience into striking new arrangements. "Good artists borrow," goes perhaps the pithiest version of this position, alternately attributed to T. S. Eliot, Picasso, and Steve Jobs. "Great artists steal."

It's obvious that an enormous amount of cultural production is recombination. Composers write new work based on old themes. Authors patch strings of real-life episodes together to form a new story. Hollywood reboots lucrative franchises, and then reboots them again. Cover songs play from radio stations across the planet.

Some of these projects stay so close to the original that we wonder why the artist bothered to produce a new version. Some of them stray so far from the source that we wonder why the artist bothered retaining the original title.

But despite variations in ambition and quality, some projects of recombination—Shakespeare's *Antony and Cleopatra*, Beethoven's reworkings of Scottish and Russian folk melodies, Beyonce's adaptation of Warsan Shire's poetry in her visual album *Lemonade*—clearly rise to the level of art.

It's also clear that the basic elements of the world function as food or fuel for the mind. Neuroscience has identified strangeness and surprise as triggers of new ideas, echoing artists like Martha Graham, who were already well aware of the principle through personal experience: "And then there is inspiration," Graham writes. "Where does it come from? Mostly from the excitement of living. I get it from the diversity of a tree or the ripple of the sea, a bit of poetry, the sighting of a dolphin breaking the still water and moving toward me . . . anything that quickens you to the instant."

The world is the raw material of every artist. Experience is an element of creation, just as much as a painter's paints or a writer's pen. The richness and variety of a life can contribute to the richness and variety of the textures an artist brings to their work.

But if the fundamental spark of creation is the material world, we'd expect to see a clear relationship between experience and creation: the more you see, the more you make.

Instead, many people who see marvelous things never create anything. In fact, constant consumption of new experiences can distract from creation. Past a certain point, experience becomes overwhelming. It doesn't lead to more creation, but to exhaustion and paralysis.

Artists with the richest and most varied experience of the world do not always, or even usually, make the greatest work. Some artists crisscross the globe with notebooks, easels, and more-or-less-willing companions in tow, on the trail of experience that will spark inspiration.

But from a single room in her childhood home, Emily Dickinson composed one of the most remarkable bodies of poetry in any language.

Some people can stand in a great cathedral without discovering a single new idea. Some can stand in a New England garden and discover that it's a cathedral.

We often have the illusion that some element of the world—a stream, or face, or street—prompts inspiration. Instead, it may be that inspiration itself chooses that stream, or face, or street to show the artist, illuminating it among all others.

But over time, the world wears out. We return again and again to the same stream, face, corner—and each time, it gives us a little less. The problem isn't that the object never changes: no face or stream is ever twice the same. And the problem isn't that the object always changes: we can listen to an identical recording of a single song again and again.

But however potent, any object will eventually lose its ability to move us.

The more frequently we seek it, the faster the loss.

We may continue to return to a place, an object, or a memory from nostalgia, for comfort, out of loyalty or habit. Our appreciation and our understanding of it may deepen with time.

But it will never retain its original power over us—especially not its power to spur us to create.

INCARNATION AND ART

Over the long span of history, the things we create have become a world of their own.

This has produced a variant of the old theme that art is simply imitation. Inspiration doesn't just come from the world, this story goes. It comes from art itself.

To some degree, the idea that art flows from art is a simple truth. Almost all art is inflected by earlier art, whether an artist works to imitate previous work or reject it. Even the art forms that draw most directly from the natural world, like still lives or death masks, are created in the context of other still lives or death masks. So it's easy to mistake the obvious influence of art on art for inspiration itself.

The misconception that art is the source of art can result in agonizingly self-referential art scenes. Images are deliberately indecipherable without the context of a larger conversation between a rarefied few. Literature descends into little more than carefully curated displays of erudition and in-jokes. Buildings are constructed not primarily to shelter, comfort, or delight, but as arguments against other buildings.

But the idea that art is the source of art has traction even outside elitist art scenes. It also appears in some of the most familiar advice given to artists: to get familiar with our contemporaries, and crib from the greats.

"You must learn the history of art," professors warn, "or the only things you make will be monuments to your own ignorance."

This is good advice. All artists can learn an enormous amount from what has been created before, and what is being made right now. We can discover possibilities we never even dreamed about, find companions among artists we will never meet, begin to understand what thoughts have already been talked to death, and what borders have never been crossed yet.

Understanding the contemporary art world can also help an artist find her audience. Whole careers can be built by savvy guesswork about the spirit of the times, or skillful imitation of the greats. Imitation is also a fundamental way artists develop technique.

But cribbing from the greats doesn't answer the all-important question of what inspired the greats themselves. Why has all the source material for Shakespeare never resulted in other Shakespeares, either before or since? Why have none of the thousands of students who read Ralph Ellison each year ever produced another American novel on the scale of *Invisible Man*?

The artists who usher in new eras, the greats we reach back to imitate, cannot be explained solely by imitation or recombination.

They are almost always well-versed in the history of their field. They know its rules and accomplishments. They're up-to-date on their contemporaries. Marvin Gaye, for instance, was deeply rooted in longstanding gospel and soul traditions. He was well connected in the contemporary pop scene. But his late solo work wasn't simply the next obvious step in those traditions, any more than it was the next obvious step for the mainstream music of his time. His work represented both a culmination of history, and a clean break with it.

Some might argue that artists who seem iconoclastic, like Gaye, or Walt Whitman, are actually just the first in their time to respond to broad shifts in culture and technology. And perhaps it was only a matter of time before a white artist, like Elvis Presley, hit it big selling the sound of blues and gospel created by generations of Black artists before him.

But as Griel Marcus points out in *Mystery Train*, no white artist successfully broke the racial taboos in mainstream American culture before Presley. And despite a host of imitators, no one successfully replaced Presley in his lifetime. Fourth-century Hippo and Brooklyn after the Civil War were both world centers in great foment, ripe for the creation of new culture. But Hippo only produced one Augustine, and Brooklyn only produced one Walt Whitman.

Some individual artists, like Whitman, or Bob Dylan, or Bob Marley, lay groundwork for whole new forms of art: the free verse poem, the singer-songwriter, the reggae movement.

But even when a single artist influences thousands more, no artist ever creates solely by imitation.

In fact, the artists whose influence is most recognizable, like Dylan, are also the most difficult to duplicate. Most wedding singers can passably mimic the average pop star, and most competent songwriters can knock out a harmless ditty in any genre—including a Dylan satire.

But even other great songwriters would have trouble forging a song that could genuinely pass for Dylan. It's always obvious when a songwriter owes something to Dylan—and just as obvious that that songwriter isn't him.

An artist can mimic the outward signs of another artist's genuine encounter with inspiration. But although that kind of mimicry may manipulate an audience, it does not genuinely move them. The more precise the imitation, the clearer this becomes.

The weird accuracy of an Elvis impersonator only serves to underscore the unique power of Presley's own performances. We may be dazzled by the precision of the mimicry. But not even the most enthusiastic tourist mistakes it for art.

The figures we are told to imitate did not arrive at their own art by imitation.

And our attempts to imitate them will never result in art.

We can learn from them about craft: how to draw a better line, write a better sentence, structure a better song.

But the fundamental lesson they have to teach us is not how to create like them, but that we can never create like them. They do not show us how to be more like they are, but how to be more true to ourselves.

If we want to create, we need to turn not to the world of art, but to the voice that called it into being, and not to any other artist, but to the voice of inspiration that leads all artists on.

INCARNATION AND THE HUMAN MUSE

The history of art is littered with artists whose work fixates on the form or personality of an actual person, a category we've come to call *muse*.

Dante Gabriel Rosetti famously painted the flaming redhead Elizabeth Siddal on canvas after canvas. Film director Alfred Hitchcock returned to the same actresses again and again, with frightening intensity. And Eminem's references to his ex-wife, Kim, have given her almost as much notoriety as him.

Artists form all kinds of collaborations with each other, to exchange ideas and share work. But a muse is not a collaborator. Their only role is to provide inspiration.

For the muse, this position is strange, and often profoundly uncomfortable. Muses are told, and may believe, that they are vital to an artist's work. But they have no control over it.

A muse's image or speech may take center stage, again and again, in an artist's creations. But when credit or compensation is involved, the tune changes. A muse may occasionally be rewarded in the form of a movie role or modeling fee. But in general they are expected to render whatever service they provide the artist absolutely free. Their name never appears along with the artist's on the author page or the corner of a canvas. It's the artist who accepts payment and prestige from galleries, publishers, and audiences.

Wiser or more skittish individuals may reject the role of muse completely, like Helen Mirren, who refused Hitchcock's advances, both personal and professional.

Others fall into the role of muse but strain to develop their own voice beyond it. F. Scott Fitzgerald's wife, Zelda, didn't simply activate his imagination. She had her own talents, and independent flashes of inspiration. And like countless other artists before him, Scott folded some artifacts of her inspiration into his work under his name: a form of uncredited collaboration, a breed of journalism—or perhaps straight plagiarism.

An artist could argue that a muse would never have turned those flashes of inspiration to art. And that may be true. But at heart, artists know that the living quality of art flows not from our expertise but from the presence of inspiration, which is what makes some of us willing to resort to theft when we discover it unguarded.

Picasso had a tendency to fixate on other working artists as his muses—which often proved dangerous to their own artistic life. He painted his lover, the surrealist photographer Dora Maar, on his famous canvas *The Weeping Woman*, and many others. But he also encouraged her to close her renowned photography studio at the height of its popularity. After they parted ways, her career never recovered.

Another muse of Picasso's, Françoise Gilot, was a working artist before she became his lover and the subject of many of his paintings. But after she left him, he tried to prevent galleries from acquiring her work, causing her lasting professional damage. To regain control over her own image, Gilot responded with self-portraits, commenting that "one's ego is not satisfied by the fact that one has been painted by Picasso."

The attention an artist turns on a muse can be intoxicating. But it is not the attention of selfless love. An artist may care for a muse as a person, and vice versa. But concern for the well-being of the muse is never the central dynamic between artist and muse. The artist's impulse with a human muse is at best to capture and enshrine, at worst to lay bare and consume—never to nurture.

And this is not simply a masculine reaction to a feminine presence: people of any gender are just as susceptible to this dynamic.

Artists can become so fixated on their idea of a muse that the person's natural growth or change feels like tragedy to the artist. Lewis Carroll mourned as the little girl he wrote his Alice cycle for grew into a woman.

And some artists actually try to prevent a muse's growth or escape. After a falling out, Hitchcock kept the actress Tippi Hedren, who had starred in both *Marnie* and *The Birds*, under contract for two full years, paying her every week not to work, rather than let another director employ her.

The fact that an artist feels hunger for a muse may cause them to believe that they are the ones who are suffering. But no matter how hungry we may be, the artist is never the one who is in danger of being consumed.

The attention an artist gives a muse is occasionally platonic. But more often, it's confused with romantic longing, physical desire, or both. Whether that attraction is ever satisfied or not, the confusion can be disastrous for everyone involved.

Artists who believe a lover is also the source of our art may tolerate a relationship we would never otherwise accept, for the sake of our work.

We may unfairly demand that a lover go to the same lengths and make the same sacrifices that we do for our art.

And when an artist believes a lover is the source of their inspiration, the death of that relationship doesn't just threaten a season of heartbreak. It seems to strike at the core of our ability to create.

These burdens, added to the profound snarl of expectation and emotion in any deep human connection, make it very difficult for any relationship on these terms to survive.

"One face looks out from all his canvases," Christina Rosetti writes in "In an Artist's Studio," a poem about her brother's fascination with his model and lover Elizabeth Siddal. "He feeds upon her face by day and night. . . . And she with true kind eyes looks back at him . . . not wan with waiting, not with sorrow dim; not as she is, but was when hope was bright; not as she is, but as she fills his dream."

This total attention that never leads to understanding, this act of laying oneself bare without ever being known, can cause profound vertigo for the muse, especially if either the muse or the artist has mistaken the intensity of the artist's attention for love.

The muse, once showered with what felt like adoration, now finds herself shunted aside as the director peers up at an image of her that flickers on a screen, totally uninterested in the actual woman still beside him. She has suffered the bizarre indignity of losing a lover to her own image.

And although the artist's rendering of the muse may become familiar around the world, the muse may recognize no trace of her real self in it.

This image of the human muse, ignored as the director splices together endless frames of their face, is the central argument against the idea that artists ever find the true source of inspiration in another person.

Because at the actual moment of creation, the muse is excluded: a bystander, at best. They never move the brush or splice the film—precisely because they are not, in fact, the inspiration.

When we turn to the actual men and women who appear in an artist's work, we don't find a satisfactory explanation for the art they seem to inspire.

In the centuries since Dante wrote the *Commedia*, a whole industry of literary historians investigated his real-life contemporaries. Dante's treatment of them is epic and unforgettable. The politician Ugolino is condemned by Dante to gnaw at the back of his enemy Ruggieri's head for all time. The adulterous lovers Francesca and Paolo are punished by an embrace that becomes a hell as it stretches into eternity.

But nothing about the *Commedia*'s real-life models suggests that they carried within themselves the seeds of one of the world's most enduring pieces of art.

Ugolino and Ruggieri were villains, but not extraordinary villains. Political betrayals like theirs occur daily, around the world. But they don't give rise to art like the *Commedia*.

Paolo and Francesca's story is compelling. Forced by her father to marry a nobleman she reviles, Francesca embarks on an affair with his handsome brother, Paolo, until both she and Paolo are killed by her outraged husband.

But the world has produced countless other romances with similar quantities of blood and pathos, probably even in thirteenth-century Florence. And none of them provoked an artistic response equal to the *Commedia*.

In fact, when we compare the figures immortalized in the *Commedia* to similar events in history, what becomes most remarkable about the *Commedia*'s real-life models is just how ordinary they begin to seem: just another pair of corrupt politicians, just one more episode of adultery that ends in violence.

Their familiarity is strikingly at odds with the profound originality of the *Commedia*.

Furthermore, no human muse activates all artists. The same figure who might spur one artist to fill reels of film or reams of pages leaves another artist cold.

Hitchcock found Hedren magnetic. But her presence wasn't a requirement for other great directors of the time, who managed to produce lasting work without her. And when she worked with other directors, her simple presence didn't magically spark the production of Hitchcock-quality films. (In fact, Hedren holds the distinction of having worked as an actress with both Hitchcock, known as one of film's best directors, and Ed Wood Jr., affectionately known as one of the worst.)

If Paolo and Francesca, Ugolino and Ruggieri, Kim Mathers or Elizabeth Siddal carried some special ingredient of art in themselves, we would expect to see other great works break forth in their orbit. But none did.

A handful of people, usually fixtures in a thriving art scene, are photographed and painted, captured in poems or songs by multiple artists. But none of them prompt creation in every artist they meet.

Even a profound and productive connection between an artist and a human muse rarely lasts for the artist's entire creative life. Many of the artists most famously linked with human muses also have a strong tendency to drift from muse to muse. Hitchcock "discovered" Hedren in an attempt to replace Grace Kelly, who he'd already featured in three earlier movies—and alienated with his abuse. And as Elizabeth Siddal lay dying, Dante Gabriel Rosetti snuck out for trysts with Fanny Cornforth, an artist's model who would become his next muse.

Most significantly, the end of a relationship with a muse doesn't always interrupt an artist's work. If anything, it's the art that remains constant in the lives of these artists, despite an ever-shifting array of supposedly indispensable muses.

A human muse may seem to trigger inspiration. But in fact, what a muse triggers is a highly personal reaction in an individual artist. That reaction may take many forms: desire, longing, a sense of safety, even anger. But whatever the reaction, it serves the same basic function: to disarm our conscious defenses, so that we can hear the voice of inspiration.

And when we compare art to its actual subjects, what seems most remarkable is never the subject itself, but the power of art to transform any ordinary thing caught in the blast space of the creative exchange between the artist and inspiration.

THE PARADOX OF INCARNATION

It's hard to understand how Dante Gabriel Rosetti could paint idealized images of Siddal all day and betray her the same night. Or how Johnny Cash could write the enduring hymn to fidelity "I Walk the Line" for a wife he famously left for another woman.

Cash may have been prompted to make the promises of "I Walk the Line" because of his own doubts about whether he could keep them. And as Siddal lay dying, Rosetti may have preferred to remember her as she had been, not as she was.

But both men—and many other artists—produced art that fully transcended anything they could personally achieve in life.

This is the paradox of incarnation in art. Art bears all the traces of our circumstances and limits. But it also bears witness to the spirit that carries art into the world through us: a God capable of true fidelity, bearing incorruptible beauty, strong enough to keep promises of eternity.

The wild claims of love songs, directed from any person to another, are absurd. No matter how sincere, they're never credible. The stock-in-trade of love lyrics is the absolute and the impossible.

We do occasionally see examples of extraordinary commitment and sacrifice between lovers. But the lyrics of love songs rarely reflect the blend of revelation and deception, generosity and selfishness, fear, betrayal, delight, desire, inertia, and accommodation that mark most human connections.

Instead, our poems and songs enshrine a love only a god could offer or withstand: pure, total, endless. Misplaced in a pop song, promises of this love function as a kind of clumsy idolatry. But they also serve as signs of God: both clues to God's identity, and of our need for that quality of love, which we don't learn from any example in this world, but only by our own desire for it.

In the same way, no portrait ever records only one face. It also records the image of God in the faces of all people.

This is why the object of the poem, the song, the image, always seems insufficient to explain art's power.

And why abstract art, which seems to make no reference to any object, can carry the same power, or even more.

No art is ever simply a response to an object. The act of creation is not just an amplification of any human emotion—love, curiosity, despair, or ecstasy, ratcheted up to a level so high it begins to leave traces on the page or tape.

Art bears traces of all of these, but is also a completely distinct category: the evidence of a direct encounter with the source of all creation.

THE SELF AS SOURCE

The only element that is available to every artist, but no one else, is ourselves.

This fact, combined with the sense that inspiration speaks from deep in the mind's secret recesses, can lead to another illusion: that the artist is the source of art.

According to this theory, the artist's primary material is our own personality—the furniture of our mind, the architecture of our anxieties, our diseases, obsessions, hopes, dreams, and limits, along with the sum or inversion of our experience.

"The painter, the sculptor, the composer, the epic rhapsodist, the orator, all partake of one desire," Emerson writes, "namely to express themselves."

Less egocentric versions of this theory hold that even the smallest events of an individual life, observed with unflinching honesty, take on universal resonance. It's an almost incarnational claim, that an individual can both contain and reveal the universal.

In a 1938 letter to his teenage daughter, F. Scott Fitzgerald offers a memorable version of this view: "You've got to sell your heart, your strongest reactions, not the little minor things that only touch you lightly. . . . It was necessary for Dickens to put into Oliver Twist the child's passionate resentment at being abused and starved that had haunted his whole childhood. . . . This is especially true when you begin to write, when you have not yet developed the tricks of interesting people on paper, when you have none of the technique which it takes time to learn. When, in short, you have only your emotions to sell."

Entire schools of art are based on this theory, like Method Acting, which trains actors to equip the characters they play with emotions mined directly from their own history. The first of the three creeds of the Beat Generation, as summed up by Lucien Carr, states that "naked self-expression is the seed of creativity." And in *Picasso Baby*, Jay-Z agrees with them: "Rap is thinking out loud, and you putting your fears and your vulnerabilities and your insecurities to music."

Significantly, Fitzgerald's advice is impossible *not* to follow. No artist can avoid introducing ourselves into our art, because art only emerges when inspiration becomes incarnate, expressed through the artist, and clothed in the experiences, materials, and culture that are available to us. Even artists who work to erase themselves from their work leave clues to themselves in those erasures.

The idea that the source of art can be found in the life or character of the artist is also attractive to everyone from professors of literature to Taylor Swift fans, which means that millions of pages have been devoted to cataloging the detritus of artists' lives, in both learned monographs and online fanzines, in search of the source of their art.

But all of this only serves to highlight how fully art transcends the details of any artist's life.

This becomes excruciatingly clear when we hear a songwriter or actor struggle through a press junket. No matter how charming the artist, or how revealing they're prepared to be, the details of their lives never have the impact of seeing the musician play or the actor act. Childhood stories, adult meditations, the intricacies of who knew who in which scene, never come close to conveying or explaining the power of art itself. The more a musician talks about himself, the more we wish he'd sing.

We can learn an enormous amount by studying other artists.

We can begin to recognize what a person looks like in the grip of inspiration, how other artists negotiate with it, and what they've accomplished.

We can gain courage by the risks another artist took, learn new techniques for laying paint on canvas or configuring amps, take note of which books our heroes read and what kind of education they did or didn't have.

But art can't be explained by any sum of the individual who created it, either the smallest details of that artist's life, or its most potent emotional events.

Crime and Punishment reflects Dostoyevsky's lifelong fascination with crime tabloids, but millions of other Russians read those without producing even a chapter of *Crime and Punishment*. The death of John Lennon's mother influenced his songwriting for decades, but no other boys who lost their mother in England that year grew up to be John Lennon. Even academic biographers armed with letters, diaries, and interviews with both an artist and her intimates can't reliably pinpoint the source of art in the individual, or the recipe to produce even one more page of her work.

Searching the caves of an artist's personality for the source for art is an intellectual dead end. In the academy, it ultimately proved so fruitless that some new movements deny an artist's life has any bearing on their art, a counterargument almost as unsupportable as the original idea.

But Fitzgerald was right about one thing: what will sell.

As he promised, self-expression today sells everything from memoir, to tabloids, to reality television. Around the globe, on countless social media platforms, people reveal their deepest responses to life: sometimes earnestly, sometimes inadvertently, sometimes desperately. They provide millions of test cases for the idea that self-expression is the root of art.

And they produce virtually no art.

Maybe this is because only a special few, very different from the rest of us, are capable of creating art. When non-artists express themselves, we hear noise. When artists express themselves, we see art.

But social media and reality television include many established artists, deeply committed to self-expression. If art is fundamentally a matter of artists expressing themselves, we'd expect at least some of this activity to produce art. It does not.

Maybe this is because the expression is dishonest. Some "revelations" of social media and reality TV are unmistakably manipulative and cynical.

But some are so raw it's lacerating.

And none of it rises to the level of art.

The recipe for art that Fitzgerald gives his daughter—to probe the deepest springs of her own emotions—has another definition: therapy.

Art is clearly a powerful therapeutic tool. Elderly patients who have not spoken in years burst into song when they hear the strains of music from their youth. Children who are barely verbal express deep emotion, and deep insight, when encouraged to dance or draw.

And creation can work as therapy: a way to explore, understand, and release elements of our identity, history, and reality.

But the millions of hours people spend in therapy rarely result in art—even when the patient is an artist.

Therapy can clear blocks to creation, help artists create lives that support creation, and give insights that flow into our art. It can save our lives, so that we're still around to create.

But it is almost never the site of creation.

The idea of art as self-expression has the most traction in art forms that center on story, like fiction, songwriting, and theater. The imprint of the artist leaves the clearest mark in these genres, because we see the actor herself on stage and learn details of a singer's life from their song.

But in music, architecture, or abstract art, it's much more difficult to argue that art is simply an expression of the artist: that the main themes of a Beethoven sonata are a logical result of his emotions or experiences. And to advise an architect that all she has to sell are her own emotions verges on nonsense.

Some part of us is always bound up in what we create, as inspiration becomes incarnate in the materials and circumstances of our unique lives.

It's useful to us to know ourselves, so we can tell the difference between our habits or obsessions, and true inspiration. And so that we can welcome the full spectrum of ourselves as we create.

But self-expression is not a satisfying explanation for the source of art.

The most damaging variation of the idea that art flows from the artist is the illusion that art flows from an artist's wounds.

It's no secret that heartache spurs creation.

The principle is familiar to any high school kid who ever scrawled out a clumsy poem in response to their first broken heart. Even in established artists, wounds sometimes seem to prompt artistic leaps. And some artists are willing to contemplate an eternity of pain in exchange for that kind of reward.

Why does pain, which can sap an artist's strength, break our concentration, and stunt our practice, sometimes result instead in outpourings of creation?

Because pain weakens our wills, which allows the flow of inspiration that has always been present: unseen, ignored, or even forcibly subdued in favor of work that seemed to have more immediate reward—or demanded less risk or sacrifice.

Pain can strip us of defenses and pretense that may have protected us—or held us back—for our entire life. We don't create by choice, but necessity: no longer what we *can* make, but what we *must*, in order to survive.

Artists prompted by pain respond with almost infinite variety. Some bear witness to suffering with excruciating detail. Others exaggerate it, transforming childhood fears into the monsters of horror films. Some create works of startling beauty, either as a retreat from pain, or as an act of war against it.

But the undeniable fact that pain prompts artistic outpourings does not prove that pain is a crucial ingredient of art—or even a necessary one.

The vast majority of pain in the world does not result in acts of creation.

Pain alone does not reliably produce art.

Some people find themselves driven to create, sometimes for the first time, in the midst of trouble or grief. And what they create, even if they don't have formal training or an established artistic practice, can be compelling.

Loss and hardship may also give us other gifts that are useful for an artist: a sense that we have nothing to lose, a deep awareness of our need for something beyond ourselves.

But even among established artists, pain doesn't always prompt creation. It also derails projects, or whole careers. Pain can even leave an artist with a case of permanent creative paralysis, like Truman Capote, who was so wounded by the experience of writing *In Cold Blood* that he produced very little significant work in the years that followed, until his death.

And relying on wounds to prompt art can allow our sensitivity to other prompts, like beauty and wonder, to fade. Our work no longer contains the full range of possibilities, but only repeats a single note.

Much more important, when artists believe that our wounds are the source of our art, we may cling to sources of trauma, drama, and addiction under the illusion that these destructive elements actually form the foundation of our identity as an artist. Our refusal to heal, treasuring wounds for the sake of our art, can threaten our relationships, our own well-being—and our ability to create at all.

The clear connection between art and pain has also given rise to the impression that artists suffer more, or even feel more, than other people.

When people make this argument, they often point to the tragic personal stories of some artists: the early deaths of rock and roll stars, the suicides of the poets.

These litanies of addiction, mental illness, and bad luck are almost never balanced by stories of equally significant artists who lived long, happy, and unremarkable lives, like William Carlos Williams, who wrote his large body of poetry in the evenings after serving full days as a pediatrician, or Wallace Stevens, who produced almost all his poems while serving as a prosperous executive at a successful insurance company.

They also fail to take into account the general level of suffering in the world. All people at some point suffer loss, doubt, trouble, and pain. So artists, being human, can expect to suffer all these things as well.

Artists do sometimes suffer simply by virtue of being artists. In many cultures, the choice to devote a life to art requires a sacrifice of financial security and prestige. Some artistic disciplines demand punishing training, or a nomadic lifestyle that puts pressure on family and friendships.

But it is not at all clear that the troubles artists face are worse, or even equal to, the challenges of other professions: the miner who works all day without sunlight, the banker who works every waking hour, the maid whose back is bent from cleaning messes she didn't make.

The difference is that artists are often eloquent on the topic of our own suffering.

Sometimes when artists record our own pain, we give voice to the suffering of many others who wouldn't otherwise have a way to name what they feel.

But it can also create the illusion that artists suffer more than others, simply because artists leave behind a record of our sorrow or rage—unlike the miner, the banker, or the maid.

It's possible that the wounds we sustain in life make us more vulnerable to trouble, despair, or addiction—and also more vulnerable to inspiration. As Leonard Cohen famously claimed, it's through our cracks that light comes in.

But the fact that our cracks sometimes reveal unexpected light does not mean that inspiration cannot be present without pain.

Instead, it hints at great wells of inspiration that lie untapped in all kinds of people who would never consider searching themselves for it, until a crack reveals it.

Artists do not hurt more, or feel more, than the rest of the world. We are not uniquely fragile, or uniquely strong. We are not required to bear more weight than anyone else—or any less.

When we begin to think of ourselves as either more gifted or more wounded than the rest of the world, we make the dangerous mistake of underestimating the passions, hardships, joys, talent, and strength of all people.

And we are divorced from the foundation of our ability to touch other minds and hearts: the fact that, in the most important ways, we are just like everyone else.

This does not give us license to steal the stories or the songs of others and sell them as our own. Or to ignore the myriad stories of the world, because the only one we really need to understand is ours.

In fact, the opposite is true. When we recognize how much we have in common, we also see how much we have to learn from everyone else: all the different ways that people around the world and

through history have borne the same sorrows, celebrated the same joys, tried to solve the same problems.
　So artists, at our best, live in a world without strangers.
　We are dazzled by the world's variety.
　And we understand it by consulting our own heart—not because we believe it to be unique, but because we know it is not.

INCARNATION AND TECHNIQUE

Inspiration becomes incarnate in the materials and culture of the world that surrounds us, in the details of our circumstances, and the unique folds of our minds.

But the work we devote to shaping ourselves and our lives to welcome inspiration is also a form of incarnation.

The work of an artist takes two major forms that in practice are thoroughly entangled: the discipline to develop technique, and the discipline to create.

A technician, no matter how skilled, is not automatically an artist.

But without technique, even moments of great inspiration will not result in art.

No matter how much fire is in his heart, a dancer can't execute all the movements he imagines if he never trains. Without training, he doesn't just risk artistic failure, but injury.

A photographer may see the perfect shot, but if she doesn't understand light or framing, the photograph she gets may only serve as a memento of what was missed.

No one can hear an actor who hasn't learned to project, no matter how nuanced her performance.

A pianist who only knows a handful of chords can only make choices between a few notes. But one who knows the entire range, with all their combinations and shades, can reproduce anything that plays in their mind.

So writers apprentice to form sentences strong enough to carry the weight of great ideas. Painters begin by practicing ellipses that will form the foundation of new images. Even self-taught musicians like Dizzy Gillespie, who spent his early career playing only in the key of B flat, or Robert Johnson, who developed a completely idiosyncratic tuning when he taught himself to play guitar, are technical masters of their instruments, although that mastery may take a different form from any other player in the world.

Technique isn't just a matter of building mechanical skills—stretching, sketching, playing scales. It also describes invisible mental strength.

A songwriter doesn't just develop skill on piano or guitar. She also builds muscles for songwriting itself: confidence, daring, the ruthless ability to prune and discard, a history of her own failures and success, along with a constantly expanding library of the innovations, tricks, triumphs, and failures of every other artist she encounters.

Actors don't just memorize lines and hit their marks. They also develop an interior apparatus that allows them to change the scenery in their own minds, to sweep themselves off the stage of their own body, and to conjure another personality in their place.

And technique doesn't just give us the skill to capture inspiration as it arrives. It soberly selects and shapes the artifacts an artist produces while in inspiration's grasp.

In many ways, every artist is like a photographer, stalking the perfect moment. Technique is our camera, which allows us to capture and share the visions we've seen. We may take shots leading up to the moment. When it arrives, we may shoot from many angles. We may capture images no other photographer would see, even one who stood beside us. And we may keep shooting after the moment passes.

But a large part of our success as artists is based on our ability to pick the key moment from our contact sheet, to separate what's inspired from what's only interesting or accomplished—and then to crop away everything else.

Performers do this in advance, through rehearsal. Composers do this after the fact, through editing. But all forms of art require the ability to choose, arrange, and discard.

But displays of technique, even dazzling ones, do not constitute art. There's almost nothing less interesting than a photograph that only serves to showcase how deft a photographer is at handling equipment.

And it is far easier for inspiration without technique to connect with an audience than technique without inspiration. Poorly retold, a great story can still draw millions of people into a movie theater. Poorly played, a great song can still make people dance.

Conventional wisdom on creation holds that artists tend to fall along a spectrum between the craftsman, whose trade is pure technique, and the shaman, guided by pure inspiration. Creation, according to this line of thinking, is also divided, into moments of pure inspiration, and stretches of dull craftsmanship.

It's a convincing framework, because it describes the experience of some artists: the flash of inspiration, executed over the course of long hours, or even years.

But many artists do not simply execute a complete vision given in a single blinding flash. Instead, we're led by inspiration in a step-by-step revelation.

Inspiration is present not just when we conceive of a project, but in the midst of it: as we begin to frame a structure, give its bones flesh, and refine our vision. Along the way, we make all kinds of discoveries we never dreamed of in our first moment of inspiration. And each piece is fully revealed to us only when it is complete.

When we grow in technique, we discover that inspiration is present in moments of creation we once thought of as drudgery. As we learn the right notes, we discover another way to sing the song. In editing the lines of a story, we unearth a new beginning.

And when mature technique forms, the tension between technique and inspiration sometimes dissolves completely. More and more of our work emerges fully formed, eliminating much of the conscious process of editing. The poet who struggled over each line in youth begins to receive whole poems in single blasts.

Still, as Stanislavski, the father of Method Acting, observes, the more talent you have, the more technique you need. In fact, the barb of inspiration is often what drives an artist to develop the technique to match it, to become equal to the things we hear and see.

This is the purpose of technique: to allow an artist to respond to inspiration with perfect freedom.

Technique does not call inspiration forth, but releases it.

Technique is always a servant of inspiration. Without inspiration, technique has nothing to express.

But technique doesn't just give us the tools to execute our vision. It also shapes us in ways that make us more receptive to inspiration.

The self-control that helps us to hold a note in tune allows us to tune ourselves to inspiration. The familiarity we build with our own voice helps us to recognize the voice of inspiration.

Earning technique requires constant confrontation with our mental and physical limits. And confrontation with our limits builds the humility we need to follow a voice that is not our own, and the confidence to act without hesitation as inspiration leads us on.

Ultimately, technique can be seen as an act of devotion, a sign of the value we place on our art, measured by time we spend and sacrifices we make as we shape our bodies and minds in the service of inspiration.

INCARNATION AND DISCIPLINE

The world offers a great deal of external pressure to develop technique: everything from parents insisting middle-class kids practice their scales, to art schools that offer students a complete pattern for life, with constant external prompts and consequences.

And the development of technique often has a clear pattern: a series of steps others have also climbed, in more or less the same order, toward the same goal.

But to make art, another kind of discipline is needed: the discipline to create.

To confront the blank page or the empty stage, day after day, and to do what only we can do, or say what only we can say.

To create, we must step out, again and again, into unmapped territory, totally uncertain of what we will find or accomplish.

It's a task that is far more daunting than the patient development of technique, no matter how demanding that technique may be.

So alongside the disciplines that build technique—sketching, learning chords, drilling dance moves—we also develop our own rituals or disciplines to create.

The first requirement for creation is simply to show up.

Raymond Carver describes this as "being at your station."

Poet Li-Young Lee frames it as asking a question, "Is there a word from the Lord?"

Jack London's stance is typically aggressive: "Don't loaf and invite inspiration; light out after it with a club."

Some artists make space to create by diligently carving out time in the pattern of an ordinary life. Others refuse to participate in ordinary life at all.

Our disciplines to create may vary wildly—everything from the musician who stumbles into rehearsal despite the excesses of the previous night, to the poet who churns out precise lines in the earliest hours of each new morning.

But carving out time to create is the foundational discipline of an artist's life.

We can't produce art if we never approach the canvas or piano bench. We can't paint while playing a video game, write while adding a column of numbers, play a song while taking an order.

If we don't make time to create, no amount of inspiration, talent, or technique will result in art.

Our state when we arrive at the moment of creation also has a profound effect on our art.

If we're high, tired, worried, or hungry when we get to the theater or pick up our pen, we may only be able to hear fragments of the inspiration we can catch when our minds are strong and clear.

And the distractions that drown out inspiration can also make us slow, rushed, or sloppy when we turn to the work of creation.

Trouble and exhaustion may open us up to encounters with inspiration. But they can also drown the voice of inspiration out. Over time, they can make it difficult for us to hear or do anything at all.

But even the artist with impeccable technique, rested, fresh-scrubbed, well-fed, and happy, is at a loss without the element of inspiration.

That fact can be so frightening that many artists never fully prepare ourselves to create. We never give ourselves quite enough time, quite enough space, quite enough sleep. This allows us to cling to the illusion of control. As long as there's something we never do, we can pretend everything would change if we just did it.

When we fully prepare—fight for technique and time, for a stable life and a clear mind—we also recognize how fully inspiration remains beyond our command or understanding.

Primed and ready, we can work for hours or years without a flash of inspiration.

Then it may fall on us in the middle of the street, in the middle of a song, in the middle of an argument, when we don't even have a pen to scrawl it down.

But although inspiration always remains stubbornly beyond our control, it does follow this strong pattern: the more an artist works, the more inspiration arrives, both in the places we expect to see it, and in places we don't.

THE MYTH OF WORK

The relationship between discipline and inspiration is so strong that it's easy for an artist to believe that, as composer John Cage says, "out of the work comes the work."

Painter Chuck Close echoes Cage in a quote that's become a common Internet meme: "Inspiration is for amateurs. The rest of us just show up and get to work."

It's a script that's especially common among men, perhaps because it positions art as a respectable, honest profession, a matter of work and discipline, not unpredictable, involuntary possession. Seeing art as simply a variety of work puts it on a par with laying asphalt or performing surgery. And that gives the artist the dignity of a construction worker or a surgeon, and helps them shed the stereotype of the impractical or lazy dreamer.

Songwriter Irving Berlin, who wrote "Puttin' on the Ritz," "Blue Skies," "God Bless America," and "White Christmas," also liked to claim that his process was nothing more than simple work: "Usually, writing songs is a matter of having to pay bills and sitting down to make the money to pay them with."

But he also admitted, "very often ideas occur to me when I'm not hunting for them." In fact, Berlin drew a clear distinction between "forced efforts," which he called "square songs," and "round songs," where "the song is just there." And he described "White Christmas," one of the most recorded songs in human history, as being "as round a song as he'd ever written."

Still, the relationship between discipline and inspiration is predictable enough that rafts of books claim to demystify inspiration with simple habits or tricks, everything from daily creative appointments to office treadmills.

Many of these techniques actually work, although none of them work consistently enough to qualify as laws: people may have more ideas while taking a walk, but not everyone who takes a walk has a new idea.

Some schools of art have also developed disciplines to welcome inspiration, like brainstorming, free-writing, and the "yes, and" of improvisational comedy, where performers aren't allowed to contradict one another, but only build from the last statement made, heaping new idea on new idea.

Over time, each artist also discovers what unique conditions help us to create: how much space, time, rest or silence we need, what materials we should always keep close at hand, what small distractions or rewards work for us.

Among all the disciplines to spur creation, the deadline may be the most common.

Some of the world's foundational works of art have been created on deadline, including Rodin's *Burghers of Calais*, Rembrandt's commissioned portraits, Bach's *St. Matthew Passion*, which was performed according to the church calendar, and Shakespeare's plays, which were written at breakneck speed to meet the demands of the theatrical season.

"Which comes first, the words or the music?" someone once asked songwriter Sammy Cahn, who penned the jazz standards "Call Me Irresponsible" and "Imagination."

"The phone call," he answered.

But relying solely on deadlines to spur creation poses dangers, both for the art and the artist.

The pressure of a deadline can help an artist get something done. But one of an artist's greatest gifts—or weapons—is time: to dream and plot, to play and fail, to create, to step away, to forget and discover, to change, to return, bringing something new, seeing things in a different way.

Deadlines can leave artists without the time to bring a piece forth fully formed—and without the flexibility to fix even simple flaws.

The state of emergency provoked by deadlines also requires recovery time that healthy creative rhythms do not. And that recovery time often cancels out the seeming productivity of a deadline-induced creative burst.

Overwork on deadline can even leave an artist with lasting damage. Musicians and dancers guard against physical strain that might rob them of their ability to perform. But mental or spiritual strain, although we can't currently measure it with the same precision, can reshape or break an artist as well.

But the fundamental problem with deadlines is that they come from outside us, spurring us to meet the demands of someone else. That's true whether we play to the lowest common denominator in a Hollywood blockbuster, or the narrow vision of a high-brow patron.

Those external pressures sometimes stretch an artist and enrich our art. But they can also confine us to a much smaller territory than inspiration would lead us to range on our own.

Deadlines may help us create individual pieces: prepare for a performance, or even write a poem. But they rarely help an artist develop a full and coherent body of art.

We don't become dancers or poets on deadline.

Most important, the world cannot set a deadline for something it doesn't know it needs. If Emily Dickinson, Fernando Pessoa, Nas, Dolly Parton, Dante Alighieri, Robert Johnson, Mary Cassat, or Vincent van Gogh had waited for someone to give them a deadline in order to create, we wouldn't have their work.

There are not enough deadlines in the world for all artists to depend on them as the spur to creation. The world simply doesn't provide enough external pressure to make art.

New voices and movements don't emerge in response to deadlines. They arrive when artists follow the voice of inspiration, regardless of what the world thinks it wants.

Because what the world thinks it wants is almost never what it really needs.

If we want to be artists, if we want to build a true body of work, the will to create has to come from within ourselves, where no cancelled contract can turn it off, and where inspiration gives us assignments that no one else could ask for or imagine, until we bring them into the world.

The discipline to create also has a counterfeit: a stubbornness or buoyancy in the face of setbacks that can carry a person far, in the art world or life—even in the absence of talent, technique, or inspiration.

Often, what seems to be strength of will is actually rooted in a profound anxiety. The person doesn't work for love of the work, or in service to a vision, but because they're terrified to stop.

Because they speak constantly, they may be considered poets. Or they may be considered musicians because they won't stop singing. But since they can't bear to listen, they can offer almost no insight about this world, let alone tolerate the uncertainty required to hear and respond to the still, small voice of inspiration.

We're all familiar with artists who churn out canvases, authors who churn out books, and musicians who put out songs with astonishing rates of activity—and very little evidence of inspiration.

But even artists who listen for the voice of inspiration with patience, passion, and discipline do not always hear it. Many artists have seen pieces grind to a halt for lack of inspiration, despite the enormous amounts of time and heart we've poured into them.

In the spiritual life, empty religious practices can become a barrier to a true meeting with God. When we're sure we already know where God is found and what God wants, we can look blindly past where God actually is. So we offer worship or service to memories or shadows, not a living presence.

In the same way, artistic discipline can become an obstacle to inspiration. We can begin to confuse the practice of our creative rituals for creation itself.

When we continue with the same disciplines, long after they have stopped working, we may scratch the itch of our longing for inspiration without actually listening to its voice.

To share our inspiration with the world, we have to work. But we also have to let inspiration shape the way we work, and have the courage to change a comfortable or even powerful discipline, when it no longer works for us.

Our biggest artistic disappointments don't come from following the voice of inspiration, no matter how unlikely or wild.

Instead, we fail when we stubbornly work our own plan, long after we know in our hearts that we are no longer animated by inspiration's living presence.

TALENT, TECHNIQUE, AND INSPIRATION

Some artists latch onto the myth that art flows from work for another reason: they don't want anyone to accuse them of thinking that they're exceptional.

I'm not special, this script goes. *I just worked hard.*

But movie stars, who often trot out this sentiment on talk shows in lieu of actual humility, ignore the fact that they create surrounded by an apparatus full of people who put in all the same hours they do, or even more, but are not magically transformed by that work from extras or grips into movie stars.

And the theory that art results solely from work can't explain why Stevie Wonder or Mozart, as teenagers, were able to create masterworks far beyond the reach of writers twice or even three times their age.

Part of their ability stems from very early, very rigorous training. But even as children, they produced work beyond the grasp of composers who had trained, in absolute terms, for decades longer than they had.

Part of what a Mozart or a Stevie Wonder achieves can be explained by variations in talent. Some kids are taller than other kids.

That doesn't mean they'll be basketball stars, but it does give them an advantage on the court.

The same holds true in the arts.

Some pianists can reach beyond an octave. Some can't.

Some children learn melodies faster, memorize pieces faster, understand and begin to make accurate guesses at music's hidden math more quickly than the rest.

Some kids struggle to draw accurate likenesses. Some scrawl them out with their first crayons.

Often, it's talent that first leads to a child being identified as "an artist."

But a great deal of talent never results in art.

Some talent may go unused due to culture or circumstance. A man may shrug off his gift for capturing likenesses as a joke because he has not yet found the courage to call himself an artist. A woman may bury her remarkable facility with music in a lucrative business career. An artist who burns to create every day may be forced to spend her time changing sheets or flipping burgers, to support her family.

But even in art schools and art scenes, it's a well-known truism that the artists with the most talent are not always—or even usually—the ones who produce the most significant work.

Often, when we talk about "the most talented person I ever met," it's to lament that they never lived up to their ability.

"Talent is insignificant," says James Baldwin. "I know a lot of talented ruins."

Unearned talent can be a trap. An artist who can achieve pleasing results without much effort may never do the work necessary to build the mature technique or the mental strength art requires.

And an artist who isn't used to failure, because of their natural talent, may refuse to take the risks that art demands.

Poet R. P. Blackmur challenged the biographer Robert Caro along these lines when Caro was an undergraduate, in the habit of turning in rushed papers that received high marks due to his talent as a writer. "You're not going to achieve what you want to achieve," Blackmur told him, "unless you stop thinking with your fingers."

Talent can bring external encouragement or personal satisfaction that spurs an artist to develop. But an artist with talent faces a constant temptation. In moments of artistic difficulty, they can always use their talent to create a distraction, rather than waiting for inspiration's elusive voice.

They can produce the easy or pretty answer, instead of the true one.

In art schools, all students are chosen for their outstanding talent, and all of them put in roughly equivalent amounts of work. Dancers spend similar hours in the studio, and musicians spend similar hours in practice rooms. Some of them may do a bit more, and some may do slightly less. But it's rare, and sometimes physically impossible, for one student to work twice as much as everyone else.

But while all of them can draw, only some of them can see.

All of them can hit the right notes, but only some of them can sing.

Of course, work is not measured only in quantity, but by quality. Effective practice, in any craft, is not only a matter of hours spent but of the ingenuity, efficiency, and rigor of the practice.

So quality of practice is a popular explanation for artistic success, especially in art forms that require intensive development of technique, like classical music and dance.

But two artists who both practice with what seems to be complete commitment will still achieve radically different results. And despite the natural advantages of collecting talented people and giving them time to concentrate on their craft, top schools do not reliably produce the world's most important artists.

Expertise in an art form does not reliably lead to creation. Great writers are frequently voracious readers, but few voracious readers ever become great writers. Great songwriters are often avid music fans, but few avid music fans become great songwriters, or even great guitarists. And a great guitarist's technical ability doesn't always mean they'll give a great performance—or that they can write a song.

Rigorous training may provide an artist with the tools to fully express their inspiration. But it may also snuff the spark of inspiration out.

Some childhood prodigies go on to become Mozart. Some refuse to even own an instrument as an adult.

The limits of training are also painfully clear if we set out to build a major work of art with a blueprint drawn only from the elements we know how to train people in: technique and theory.

Bach's *St. Matthew Passion* is a near-perfect example of both theory and technique, surprising but inevitable, both sophisticated and simple, as successful as it is ambitious.

Bach was a musical expert, professional, thoughtful, and controlled. He left a clear record of his conscious choices as an artist, which are evident throughout his body of work.

"I have had to work hard," he wrote. "Anyone who works just as hard will get just as far."

But nobody has.

The *Passion* has endured for centuries, during which students have studied everything from the major themes to the intricacies of the interplay between the lyric and setting. In fact, some of those students may have a better conscious grasp of Bach's structure and choices than Bach himself did.

But it's absurd to think that any student, however well-trained, could reverse-engineer the *Passion* through painstaking application of the theory it displays.

St. Matthew Passion wasn't created in a single creative blast. It took Bach years. But many other major works enter the world fully formed, with incredible speed.

Keats left "On First Looking into Chapman's Homer" on a friend's desk at ten in the morning, after staying up talking with him until dawn. Rilke wrote the majority of his fifty-five Sonnets to Orpheus over the course of just three days. Paul McCartney wrote "Yesterday," the most widely recorded melody of its time, before breakfast. Lewis Redner woke up with the melody of "O Little Town of Bethlehem" echoing in his head. Elvis Costello wrote "The Angels Wanna Wear My Red Shoes" in ten minutes on a train out of Liverpool.

Erykah Badu freestyled her hit, "Tyrone": "I wrote all these other songs that took so much time and effort," she says, "thinking 'John Lennon will be proud of this one.' And here's 'Tyrone,' this private joke between me and God—and that's the one I'm known for."

Critics respond to these kinds of creative timelines with breathless awe because they're aware that it's impossible to consciously apply theory and technique at that speed. Something greater than technique and beyond thought spills through these artists: inspiration, the voice of God.

Inspiration is the difference between an actor who gives the tinny performance of a talented mimic, and one capable of becoming a new creature. It's the difference between a novel that does nothing more than collect deft observations and one crowded with living characters. It's the difference between a performer who hits all the right notes, and a performer who lets the song play her. It's the difference between an image that accurately reflects our world, and one that illuminates, transforms, or even dismantles it.

No matter how talented an artist is, how accomplished or how hard they worked, one of the most damning things that can be said about a piece or performance is that it was "uninspired."

Even if we only have the fuzziest definition of inspiration, the meaning here is clear: the work lacks the crucial element that makes all the artist's work, and the time and attention of the audience, worthwhile.

And work is never a substitute, let alone an explanation, for the inspiration that gives shape and meaning to an artist's work.

If work were the fundamental ingredient in art, we'd also expect to see a consistent relationship between work and art: the longer an artist works, the more successful the art.

But in the lives of artists we see very few consistent trajectories. Some burst onto the scene very young, but never repeat their early success despite decades of later work. Some work toward success more slowly, but find themselves stalled or on a downward slope, despite consistent effort.

Even artists who do build from success to success occasionally produce work of lower quality than the rest: a rotten record among a string of classics, an off night for the brilliant diva.

Interestingly, we often diagnose these failures as a symptom of the artist working "too hard."

The prescription: not more work, but more rest.

If work were the crucial element of art, we'd also expect the most grueling projects to be the most artistically successful.

Instead, novels, architecture, and theater productions that involve thousands of hours of work can end in total failure, while Paul McCartney wakes up one morning with the strains of *Yesterday* echoing unbidden in his head.

The things we work on hardest often emerge malformed and incomplete, while our best work is eerily effortless—because our best work can't be conjured by our own effort.

The relationship between discipline and inspiration is so strong that it's easy for artists, especially artists with excellent discipline, to fall victim to the idea that it is our gestures that conjure inspiration, not inspiration that conjures our gestures.

Or even that, by our gestures, we have trained or tamed inspiration.

And inspiration may seem to respond to our habits, like a wild creature that emerges from the woods each morning to collect the same handful of nuts it collected the day before.

But an artist can't, as Jack London suggests, club inspiration over the head and drag it home.

Too many artists know from experience that by the time you think you've wrestled inspiration into a cage, it's gone.

When consistent discipline leads us into consistent encounters with inspiration, it is not because we have trained or tamed inspiration.

It is because inspiration has trained and tamed us.

THE WORK OF ART

No single element—talent, work, wounds, beauty, art, personality, or even this world—can be relied on as the source of inspiration.

But the fundamental problem with believing art comes from them isn't just that it sends us looking in the wrong direction.

It's that looking to them for the source of art can blunt our capacity to receive inspiration.

It might seem like no big deal that art schools focus on technique and talent, and largely ignore inspiration. But the concentration and control that develop technique and theory can be the enemy of the surrender that welcomes inspiration.

And focus on ourselves is the opposite of the true movement that welcomes inspiration: to let go of ourselves, so something greater can come in.

Theory and technique can give us tools, and a vocabulary.

But they can't give us our own ideas.

And in the midst of creation, theory is worse than useless: it actually threatens the artist's ability to create.

"Thinking should be done beforehand and afterwards," photographer Henri Cartier-Bresson says, "never while actually taking a photograph."

At the moment of creation, any sound other than inspiration's clear voice—including our own—only clogs the channel or gums the works.

At worst, the constant noise of theory to follow, pitfalls to avoid, heroes to emulate, and competitors to best can drown out inspiration's voice completely, and paralyze the artist.

We choose how much energy we spend honing technique, and how much time we spend in creation.

We choose how hard we think and work during that time.

But none of this will produce art without inspiration, which doesn't arrive by choice or work, but as revelation.

The central activity of creation is not to think, but to pay attention, not to concentrate, but to yield, not to speak, but to listen.

The action that welcomes inspiration is surrender: the fundamental act of creation—and of both faith and love.

To surrender is not passive or weak.

In fact, there may be nothing in the artistic life, or any life, that requires more courage than to listen for the voice of inspiration without expectations, excuses, or defenses. It takes deep strength to follow inspiration regardless of what it requires, and how it may make us look, or be received by the world.

And the surrender to inspiration—to still our own voice and hands, to discard our own ambition and fears, to gaze steadily into the unknown without maps or promises—is the hardest and most important work in an artist's life.

BOOK THREE
DISCIPLINE

Most human acts are attempts to gain control. It's often our first response to any challenge, not just in art, but in life.

But control freezes us in place. And we begin to lose it in the moment we take any action, because we can never act with perfect control, and we can never perfectly control what will happen next.

Surrender, on the other hand, often results in an intense burst of action: we let go of the bank and are swept out to sea, we stop holding back our thoughts and begin to speak or sing, we cease to resist and begin to make love.

It is not wise, or safe, to surrender at random.

But it is impossible to live fully, or to create, if we never surrender at all.

THE MECHANICS OF SURRENDER

Surrender is not giving up.

Giving up can be done in solitude—we simply cease to hope or try or fight, whether anyone else is there or not.

But surrender requires an encounter with a force beyond ourselves. So whatever we fear we might lose in surrender, it also offers enormous possibility.

We are no longer in control.

But at the same time, we are in touch with a power beyond our own.

Surrender to inspiration is not the capitulation of a defeated soldier yielding to a more powerful enemy. Instead, it demands the courage of a skydiver as we step from a plane into open space. We would not be standing in the belly of the plane without training, planning, or resources. But the entire project still depends on a single step into the unknown.

In that moment, we are both freer and more helpless than we have ever been, and suddenly able to see things we could not see any other way.

We may believe it takes all our courage to step from the plane. But our courage actually grows as we fall. It doesn't grow through conscious effort. We don't make or collect courage on the way down.

But every time we stand in the belly of the plane, we discover we have more.

This is bravery in the life of an artist: not our perfect control as we attempt to scrawl our own mark on the world, but the strength to step into something greater than ourselves, to reach past what we know for what we don't.

And this is the central challenge not just in the life of an artist, but in all lives.

We know how to clench, to try, to concentrate.

The whole world, and its systems, are organized for control. The better we are at control, the better we look in the eyes of the world.

But true surrender is rare. So although it is the most crucial act in our lives, we have very little practice in it.

Talent is an accident.

Technique can be earned.

But how can we learn to surrender?

THE SPIRITUAL DISCIPLINES

The world does hold a rich collection of practices designed to help us hear and answer a voice beyond our own.

Thousands of years of humanity's best thinking and most rigorous practice in surrender reside in the spiritual disciplines.

The aim of both the artist and the believer is to develop an extremely strong will, fully applied to the project of laying down the self: the paradox at the heart of both faith and art.

The central elements of the spiritual life—silence, rest, labor, humility, poverty, community—are also central elements of the life of an artist.

Both artistic and spiritual disciplines are primarily acts of faith: that when we listen, there will be an answer, and when we wait, someone will meet us.

Both artists and mystics understand that even the simplest disciplines, spiritual or artistic, don't just carry their own rewards—they release enormous power.

And the same spiritual practices that refine a soul to hear the voice of God can also tune an artist to the voice of inspiration.

The spiritual disciplines are not blueprints by which we construct our own character, or magic tricks that bend God to our will.

They're keys that unlock the doors we've shut against the active grace and wisdom that constantly seek to make us, and the whole world, new.

And true discipline is not a matter of forcing ourselves into rigid boxes, but of learning our unique tolerances and talents, and building a life that both reflects and refines them.

A disciplined life is not the only way we can hear the voice of inspiration, or seek the face of God. In the life of the artist and the life of the spirit, both inspiration and God intrude on us even before we seek them, with acts of grace which we did nothing to earn and sometimes actively resist.

But true discipline sustains a life of creation, and a true life of any kind. Thoughtful rhythms give us the strength and the opportunity to create more, and create better, than if we work only at the mercy of chance.

With every spiritual discipline, we take just a simple step.

But it is always the skydiver's step into the sky.

And that single step doesn't just move us one step forward.

It releases us into a new world.

REST

We long for rest almost as much as we fear it.

This is one of the great paradoxes of modern life. In some parts of the world, we are freer from rote tasks than any other generation in history. Many of us no longer gather wood for our own fires or sew the seams of our own clothes. We can sift the contents of countless libraries with the stroke of a key. We travel at unimaginable speeds.

But this freedom from work has not resulted in more rest.

Instead, our lives and our minds have grown more and more crowded. As technology has freed our hands, we've invented new needs, and new work to meet them. Our leisure is filled with noise and stunts: big-screen explosions, all-terrain vehicles, bungee jumps. We don't know how to wander the natural world without a marked trail, and preferably a golf club or a gun. If we sit down, it's to watch a scrap of life even more amplified and condensed by television—or to ride a roller coaster.

We are suddenly, almost miraculously, free from the litany of repetitive tasks that have burdened every other generation. But we have lost the luxury of a farmer's long winter, the habit of siesta, the sweetness of sabbath.

We feel this loss deeply. We've all complained of being tired. We've all heard the complaint.

But our actions betray us.

The fact that we continue to avoid rest, despite the unprecedented leisure we enjoy, reveals something that until now had been obscured by all the genuine work required simply to survive in the past.

The real enemy of rest is not work. It's fear.

We're afraid to stop. We're afraid to miss out. We're afraid that if we let go for one minute, the whole creaky machine will fall apart. We're even more afraid that it will roll on merrily without us. We're afraid we won't be missed. We're afraid we don't exist, except when we do something.

Our longing for rest is fundamental, and we can't ignore it for long, even if we only allow ourselves to rest in compromised snatches. But rest, fully realized, doesn't just restore the energy we need to do more work. When we form a discipline of rest, we discover that rest is not just a need: it's a gift.

And that rest is a foundational element of creation.

The problem, we often think, is how to work more, not less.

But our ability to stop work, even in the heat of inspiration, is just as important as the will to start in the first place.

If we don't sleep, we can't dream.

At the most basic level, if we don't rest well, we don't create well. When we cheat on our sleep, our work the next day is often foggy, slow, second-rate.

Sometimes it's our passion to create that drives us on to the point of exhaustion. When we work in a white heat, we may get slightly farther than we would otherwise. But the next day, we're not as sharp. And if we persist in working past the limit of our energy, day after day, we'll begin to miss details and take wrong turns until we are thoroughly lost—or permanently harmed.

Passion is a crucial element of creation. But it can be a mask for fear.

We don't want to stop, because we're afraid the spirit that has settled on us may never return. Or because we don't know who we are apart from our work. Or because we're afraid of what might meet us in stillness.

But buildings and books can't be built at full tilt. Neither can full lives or full bodies of art. They require patience, rhythm, clarity, and a broad vision: the same things that passion and fear both compromise—and rest restores.

Inspiration can't be worn out, as God can't be worn out.

It is always speaking, but sometimes it says, "rest."

It may tell us to rest because we don't yet have the strength for what is required next, or the courage to accept it. It may tell us to rest to give us time to heal from wounds we can't even see. It may tell us to rest to remind us that inspiration is always a form of grace, not a pet that jumps on command. It may lead us into rest as a pure, simple gift. Or it may call us to rest while life reshapes us in ways we could never guess or plan.

Rest may take different forms: play, experiment, total stillness. It may last anywhere from a breath of release between lines, to years away from our craft, depending on what inspiration dictates, or our lives demand.

Part of any artist's job is to work even when we know we're not in perfect form, because we never are—and when the conditions are far from ideal, because they never are.

But the most fundamental work of an artist is to rest.

Rest is key to creation for a very practical reason: we can't create until we set aside other tasks. It's impossible to write a song while another song is playing, or to pick up a pen or brush while we hold something else in our hands. In that sense alone, rest is necessary to create.

But rest is the home of creation in a much deeper way. The true location of creation is not the moment at which we set our hand to the string, or canvas, or page. It is the moment before, when we rest, to listen for the voice that tells us what to write, or paint, or play.

The hand that moves across the page is only a mechanical response, evidence of this far more important exchange.

So our skill as creators is not measured by the strength of our hands, but by our discipline in rest.

We have been wrong about where the war is fought. We imagine we wrestle with words, paint and canvas, the notes of a song. But the real fight is in ourselves: to silence the chorus of voices that sing and threaten in our mind, to still our own voice, and to tune ourselves to the hidden one that always speaks inside it all.

Rest is far more than the simple absence of work. We don't achieve it the instant we set down our other tasks, but when our spirits settle and cease to demand, even when we have no knowledge about what comes next.

As we learn to silence ourselves, we hear the hidden voice speak.

It is only when we hear that voice that we begin to create.

So to learn to rest is the most important work we can do.

SILENCE

Artists often stake our identity on what we are able to express.

We might have some experience of the power of silence, the insights that break in when we shut out the noise of our lives.

But we don't get famous, or even paid, for the time we spend in silence. So it's easy to form the impression that an artist's first task is expression.

But it's in silence that we learn what to express. Not because silence extinguishes all sound, but because silence opens us up to so many voices the noise of life drowns out, so that we can listen to the world, to ourselves, to other people, to inspiration.

Silence can be a refuge. But we can't control silence or what it might reveal to us. So we often seek noise in order to avoid both the gifts and the demands of silence: the sorrows we lack strength to face, the revelations that make us responsible to change.

This is where our discomfort with silence comes from: not fear of the void, but of the voices that speak to us in it—both our own, and those we know could not be ours.

Without noise to distract us, we begin to hear them clearly for the first time. We start to recognize voices that before we only feared.

We learn which to argue with, which to banish, which to welcome, which to converse with all our lives.

Without a habit of silence, inspiration seems to operate on us like a lightning bolt or sneak attack. But when we develop a discipline of silence, the sound of inspiration becomes the voice of a friend—one we can pick out in the midst of a crowd, even from a scrap of conversation.

Once we form the habit, we can carry silence with us even down a busy street, or onto the stage of a crowded theater.

But even when our internal practice of silence is deep, there's no substitute for the real thing. The fact that modern life resists it so fiercely is a sign of exactly how precious it is.

True silence is both a form of deep rest and its own unique gift.

It's in silence that we hear most clearly: where we learn best how to listen, and how to speak.

SOLITUDE

To some of us, solitude may seem like one of life's rarest gifts.

To others, it's a severe punishment.

As a spiritual practice, solitude may seem like simply a more intense variety of silence.

Or something we need if we want to get any rest.

But solitude doesn't always lead to stillness or silence. In fact, it allows some of our deepest and most vital expressions.

It's only when we're alone that many of us sing, or weep, or observe ourselves naked—literally or metaphorically.

Solitude's first gift is freedom: to try, fail, or play, free from any eyes or mind but our own. It is a shelter where we can press our limits and discover possibilities that we would never dare explore in front of anyone else.

For many artists, solitude is also a practical requirement. The vast majority of artistic practice requires some solitude: we draw plans, write, paint, sculpt, practice, mostly when we're alone.

Some artists create together: film production units, groups of musicians, teams of architects, artists in shared studios, companies of dancers, writing partners, comedy troupes. But even those communal practices require a kind of corporate solitude, a deliberate retreat from the concerns of daily life, and the gaze of any audience.

Our tolerance for solitude also plays a large part in determining our technical skill: the number of hours we're willing to spend alone with a guitar, or brush, or pen in hand, singing runs, or holding the elemental positions of dance.

Solitude is distinct from silence. But we fear both for the same reason: because they leave us with few defenses against our own thoughts, or other voices that might speak to us.

Beneath the pang we feel at the threat of loneliness is the genuine terror of discovering that we are not, in fact, alone.

But for both the artist and the believer, that discovery is the ultimate goal.

We do not go into solitude to be alone, but to meet something infinitely beyond ourselves.

And in solitude, we can answer that spirit with a freedom we find nowhere else, with gestures that are new or strange, with a voice we might not otherwise recognize as our own, discovering new treasures and expressions we might never find, if we were not alone.

ATTENTION

Silence, solitude, and even rest can feel daunting, because they bring us in touch with the noise of our own minds, at the same moment that they rob us of our most comforting defenses against it.

But when we form a discipline of attention—to the world around us, and to what we hear within—we find a voice beyond the noise.

Simple attention to the material world is a potent tool against any kind of fear, including the fears that keep us from creating. It anchors us in the actual rather than the imagined, which is where fear almost always lives. And it reminds us of the depth, reality, and beauty of the world, so we can trade our imagined fears for real joy or wonder—or even inspiration.

For the artist, attention to our own rhythms can help us build practices that nurture our art: What time is best to work, for how long, in what surroundings? What patterns of sleep, eating, or life help anchor the rest of our lives?

But the spiritual discipline of attention takes a step beyond the material world. It makes no distinctions between the inner and outer worlds, but listens and watches for any change or clue in both. In fact, hints in one world often spur an artist or believer directly into the next: a voice within tells us to look up at the light pouring through the trees, and the light pouring through the trees tells us to listen to the voice that speaks to us within.

Often, attentiveness is framed as a battle to insulate ourselves against distractions, both within, and without. We pretend that we are not attentive to the world around us because of the incredible press of urgent details that compete for our attention.

But in reality, we don't usually look away from a scene or a face because something actually distracts us. Instead, we look away from beauty or pain because we can't bear to see any more. We actively seek distraction that will numb our sensations, both good and bad, because good sensations can feel just as threatening as bad ones— because they're unfamiliar to us, because they throw the rest of our lives into stark relief, or because when we hold something good in our hands, we suddenly realize we now have something to lose.

So the key to attentiveness is not building defenses against distraction.

It's cultivating the strength to truly witness the things we see.

We build that strength incrementally, first by attending to anything our mind rests on, no matter how seemingly unimportant. This expands the territory our minds are accustomed to range. And it builds the strength we need to take more in, without seeking refuge in distraction.

The more we look, the more we see. We may never have noticed the violets that line a familiar sidewalk, but when we take them in, we are overwhelmed by how many there are, and by the detail of each: the entire forest traced by veins inside every bloom. We suddenly recognize that the face of a stranger passing in the street, which a moment ago seemed like a stray detail, is in fact a whole world of its own.

Some theories hold that this is the artist's primary task, and primary talent: to pay attention. Artists are useful, according to this line, because we notice things others might not. And one of the gifts of art is that it teaches all of us new ways to attend to the world, whether we think of ourselves as artists or not.

But art isn't created when an artist simply observes our surroundings. It emerges when we let what we see shape us.

We do not know a thing best by the force of our own will. In fact, our will to know a thing can lead to its destruction: the creature torn to pieces by dissection, the mystery of love destroyed by demands for definition.

Instead, we know a thing best when we surrender to it: not when we cut a creature's heart open, but when it climbs into our lap, or when our own heart turns over as it vanishes in the distance.

And everything we are attentive to—the sigh of a dog, light among trees, song through a window, faces on the street—forms us to attend to the voice of inspiration.

The discipline of attention can even be seen as a form of prayer: listening to what God has encoded in the world, and is still speaking through it now.

Attention is not a series of solitary observations.

It is a dialogue with God.

The light through a tree tunes us to that voice. That voice turns our attention back out, to take in the uncompromising wonders of the world.

And our hope, as artist or believer, is to follow that voice through the world, and beyond.

MEDITATION

A discipline of attention expands our perception of this world.

A discipline of meditation expands our perception of our inner worlds.

It breaks apart our customary patterns of thought, our clear progressions, our quick conclusions, our confusion. In meditation, we don't solve a problem: we live with an idea.

During this long intimacy with a thought, we make discoveries we might never see if all we were looking for was an answer.

And this often leads us to better solutions—as well as new questions, that lead us out into new possibilities.

Many artists already have an almost involuntary practice of meditation or contemplation. Without our conscious control, and sometimes even against our will, our minds collect impressions and details that they then dismantle, invert, decorate, bury, resurrect, and remake, sometimes for years.

And our minds work away at all this, deep in the background, despite all kinds of storms and events in our lives.

That kind of ungoverned, secret blend of the mind's work and play will always be a central element in any artist's life.

But the conscious practice of meditation can increase the strength and flexibility of our minds and hearts, and make them more nimble, curious, and fearless in all kinds of ways, including our art.

Meditation holds a tension between two gestures that are also balanced in any creative act: concentration and surrender. We hold ourselves steady and undefended as the impressions of the world, or the contents of our own mind, flood through us. Whatever those visions or memories stir, the deepest part of us simply observes.

That steady gaze, no matter the power of the experience, is also the gaze of the artist. It's the mechanism that recognizes the chance to create, even in the midst of joy or hardship or heartbreak. It wakes the part of us that can see there might be more than pain here: there could also be a song. It reminds us that it's possible to sing, not just weep, to dance or draw, not just to speak.

Meditation often begins with this steady gaze in a storm of strong impressions. But it also builds strength to turn that gaze on a single thought, and to stay with it—not in order to bring it under our control, but to learn from and be shaped by it.

These are crucial tools for the artist: the strength to welcome a vast array of impressions but not lose ourselves in them, to choose what we will surrender to, and to set aside all distractions to make that surrender complete.

And meditation builds our strength to welcome and surrender to the unknown: both what comes from within us, and what comes from beyond.

MANUAL LABOR

When we recognize surrender as the central act of art and life, we invert traditional notions of work.

The most important work is no longer what can be measured and counted. Instead, it's internal and invisible.

Because it is hidden, this work is uncertain and demanding. We often operate without light, without guarantees or nets, and as close to the bone or the flame as we can get.

At the same time, we discover a paradox: what once seemed like labor begins to feel like relief, compared to the difficulty of our invisible internal work.

So manual labor, from monks who cultivate a monastery garden, to Borges's long walks around Buenos Aires, can serve as a form of rest.

Manual labor can lead us into rest, or create a longing for it, simply by tiring us out. But it can also accomplish tasks we think belong to rest itself. It can restore energy that has been drained by the demands of other work. And it can quiet our minds to hear the voice of inspiration.

Rote tasks of creation, like canvas prep and vocal exercises, can serve as rest from the concentration and surrender required to discover a dance or find the heart of a song.

But so can physical tasks that seem totally unrelated to creation: long swims, making meals, simple carpentry, intricate handwork, gardening.

Manual labor can even take the form of the practice of arts we're not expert in—the actor who paints in his spare time, the writer who stumbles through piano sonatas between writing chapters.

Many of our accidental experiences of inspiration happen in the midst of manual labor: as we take a shower, drive a car, wash the proverbial dishes. When we're stuck as artists, many of us turn to travel, whether it's around the block or around the world: an echo of religious pilgrimages like the great journey to Mecca, or the long walk along the Camino de Santiago, where believers seek God by taking a physical journey.

So popular wisdom for thousands of years has enthusiastically recommended manual labor to spark inspiration, all the way back to Diogenes the Cynic, who reportedly proclaimed that most problems can be solved by walking.

The advice persists because it works. Manual labor consistently unravels snarls and unearths solutions we can't arrive at by any amount of conscious effort.

We welcome inspiration not just by the motion of our minds, but by the action of our flesh—an indication of how thoroughly our own spirits are incarnate.

And even when our minds are caught in loops that seem endless, or our hearts feel frozen shut, the action of our flesh can set us free to create.

PRAYER

The central work of the spiritual life may make no sound and move nothing in this world, but still transform both the world, and us: prayer.

Most popular notions of prayer focus on our speech to God. The most common forms we see are begging and bargaining, with occasional spasms of gratitude.

But in an encounter with a god, that god's character and opinions are almost certainly more interesting than our own. If God knows everything, God must already know them. And prayer must serve some function beyond informing God of our opinions.

So the sanest form of prayer simply seeks to be with God: not to get something, but to know and be known.

This kind of prayer lays the foundation of a friendship, and it requires all the risk it takes to build real love: taking the time to know someone, not always sure what you should do, not always knowing what you want from them or they want from you, sharing who you are and what you need not because you're sure you'll get it, but because you're with someone who cares.

It's not achieved by rote repetition. But it does take showing up, time after time, through both good and bad, just like any friendship.

And it offers all the gifts of love and friendship: not a simple economic this for that, but a generosity and care that flow both ways, a desire to please and surprise on both sides. And most of all, the chance to learn another's voice by heart, and to endlessly explore the constellations of their mind.

People give us their time and attention when they listen to us. But they give us themselves when they let us listen to them. And this is the heart of any sane prayer: not just to speak, but to listen.

In prayer, the believer reaches through all things in the world, both good and bad, for God. But we do not escape the world through prayer. In fact, prayer demands an unflinching confrontation with the facts of the world, because offering half-truths to a God who knows everything is madness.

Many of us go to great lengths to avoid a direct confrontation with reality. Much of our work, and many of our prayers, are attempts to avoid it, to paper over our anxieties with words.

Looking at reality, either of the world or of ourselves, is itself a profound act of faith. Because without faith in a God who transcends what we can see, a direct encounter with the harsh conditions of this world—or our own loneliness or selfishness, our pain, or fear, or helplessness, our lack of certainty and power, even in our best moments—can be shattering, which is why we avoid it.

But prayer releases those realities to God, who holds the power to alter any reality. In prayer, we admit our own helplessness at the same moment that our encounter with God reveals it. But at the same time, God flows into those spaces, transforming them by transforming us. And since so many of the world's troubles flow from the human heart, this kind of prayer moves in the roots of that trouble, not just the symptoms.

True prayer is not a litany of demands, but an encounter of recognition, listening, and surrender: the same elements in the artist's encounter with inspiration.

And it is in this place that we may hear the still, small voice of God that is the answer and the end to all our petitions—and the spark of all art.

GRATITUDE

Gratitude finds joy in the world exactly as it is.

So it may be one of the only places where we're able to see clearly, instead of through a fog of our own desires or schemes for how the world should be different.

Some gratitude is unbidden, a spontaneous celebration.

Some must be chosen. We tune ourselves to a good that would otherwise be lost in the noise of worry or the drone of routine.

And some gratitude requires a creative act, to seek good in a place where we can't see it yet.

Without a clear object, gratitude can become an ugly exercise in self-congratulation, an opportunity for us to count our loot and marvel at our luck. It can be a way to sidestep grief and pain we desperately need to feel. Or it can function as a mask for guilt: a way for us to beat back our anxiety about how much more we have than others, without actually doing anything about it.

But gratitude also contains the idea that we've received something we did not earn. So true gratitude protects us from becoming so dazzled with some element of the world that we begin to worship it, by leading us out into the deeper mystery of who to thank.

Gratitude recognizes how little we actually control and how much we owe to others. We didn't make our own eyes, hands, voices. We didn't earn our talent. So gratitude is an exercise not just in joy, but humility.

And the fundamental gesture of gratitude is a turn to a spirit beyond ourselves: the central act in the creation of art.

Gratitude allows us to accept the world as it is. But in the same moment, it insists that the world, no matter how beautiful or awful, is never ultimate. It always points to something beyond itself: a giver, never just the gift.

And these two gifts of gratitude are also fundamental functions of art: to help us truly see our world, in the same moment that we see through it.

POVERTY AND FASTING

Some spiritual disciplines, like rest, silence, and solitude, may feel hard to find in our crowded lives.

Others, like poverty and its close relative, fasting, sometimes seem almost inescapable.

Artists often struggle to meet our basic needs, and still afford the time and materials to create.

Dostoyevsky's letters to his brother don't ruminate on the finer points of literary theory. They describe his worn-out coat and empty pockets, along with constant pleas for more funds. Rembrandt's surviving correspondence isn't about art. It's about bills—what he owes, and what he's owed. Some artists, like Alexandre Dumas or Orson Welles, become successful enough to develop a taste for luxury—and debt that compromises their freedom to create. Many others are never able to create consistently because necessity forces them to spend their entire lives in other kinds of work.

But wealth can also be a prison. It insulates the rich from the consequences of their actions—the most basic way people learn and grow. Wealth makes it difficult to get the truth. People don't lie to keep a poor man happy. But the wealthier a person becomes, the more incentive everyone has to deceive them. Wealth also attracts attention. Not many people care what a poor woman does with her money. Total strangers will attempt to influence what a rich woman does with hers. But they're not interested in who she is or what she needs—only her money.

All these basic principles of wealth hold true in the arts as well. Artists grieve the lack of resources that holds us back. But the director with a multimillion-dollar budget is among the most constrained of all artists. He can't afford to engage in the vulnerability of true community with the vast majority of people in his sphere. And even if he were willing, the vast majority of them wouldn't be. They're too busy figuring out how they can benefit from the wealth and power at his command.

Whatever his limits and blind spots, almost no one in his world will be willing to point them out to him. And the ones most willing to challenge him won't be daring him to take bigger risks to realize his inspiration. They'll be the money guys, challenging him on where exactly the cash is going, and asking for assurances that they're going to see it all again, and soon.

In many ways, the young photographer pulling out-of-date chemicals out of the art-school dumpster because she can't afford fresh ones has fewer problems—and potentially far more meaningful resources. Just about anyone in the world is willing to tell her what they really think of her work. Nobody's going to try to stop her, no matter what direction she wants to go, because nobody has risked anything on her. And the financial difficulty she faces sourcing materials may actually push aside her own preconceived ideas about the way things "should" be done, and welcome inspiration.

Not having every color of paint means we have to learn how to mix—or find entirely new materials, with entirely new possibilities—like the tradition of anonymous folk artists who build everything from elaborate crosses to tiny pianos out of matches, or Wayne Kusy's steamships made from glue and toothpicks.

Fewer possessions can also free us from the worries of ownership and the anxiety to acquire, buying us mental space that can't be had at any other price.

Poverty is not a good in and of itself. All people need basic necessities to survive, or create: food, shelter, security. The lack of any of these can give an artist clarity and perspective that we might not find in perfect comfort. But perpetual deprivation can also rob us of clarity and perspective, safety and health—and the ability to create at all.

The enormous contributions Black Americans have made to world culture also show us something else: how much was lost when millions of people were denied the resources and freedom to use their gifts during transatlantic slavery and American Jim Crow—and how much human potential is still lost in unjust systems today.

The world is much poorer for those losses. And we are all poorer every time anyone is prevented from creating by oppression or lack of resources.

The spiritual discipline of voluntary poverty, which can be an act of defiance and freedom, is distinct from the evil of involuntary poverty, which is a symptom of injustice and greed.

But for the artist, and for all of us, it's crucial to remember that wealth comes with a price, and that freedom can be found in having less.

Poverty's primary gift to the artist is not simply freedom from material pressures or constraints. It is the radical shift in perspective that comes from a refusal to participate in the constant struggle to own what everyone has, wants, or thinks we need, which completely dominates the best part of many lives.

For the believer, the call to poverty is not a call to a life of deprivation, but a way to recognize and lay claim to the riches of God. In poverty, we count our wealth in blessings like sun, rain, sky, time, love, wisdom, and inspiration: all things that no one can own, so we all own together.

We insist that they are more valuable than anything else we could claim. And we reach for spiritual richness that can't be claimed by any act in the material world, but only by the heart's unseen gestures of faith.

The treasure a believer seeks through the practice of poverty is a deeper knowledge of God, which we gain by laying aside our half-understood desires and our clumsy attempts to satisfy them. Instead, we allow God to clothe and feed us with the things God knows we need most deeply, teaching us both who God is, and who we are, by the unique quality of God's tender care for each of us.

In art, the discipline of poverty can take all kinds of forms, from an artist who is deliberately underemployed in order to have time to create, to the director who gets a show greenlit by agreeing to produce it at a fraction of the normal cost. For the blockbuster director and the arena star, who require wealth as one of their "materials," a commitment to poverty might simply be a willingness to walk out when the demands of the market begin to destroy rather than refine their vision.

Few artists start out working only for the money. If that's all a person wants, there are far faster and more surefire ways to get it than a career in art. In general, we want to make money with our art so that we have more freedom to create. But the willingness to return to the freedom in poverty can ensure an artist never works just for money, no matter how much success or hardship we face.

The embrace of poverty can also give us courage to follow the voice of inspiration even when it leads away from immediate commercial or critical success—which is often where the most significant artistic accomplishments emerge.

Any artist, however seemingly rich or poor, can also gain the clarity of freedom from wealth through fasting, the practice of temporary poverty in any area of life. An artist may fast from distraction: television, business details, social engagements. But we may also fast within our artistic practice: limit the colors in our palette, hold back from playing through a whole piece to allow it to build power, strip away the theatrical sets to get back to the story.

One of the major gifts fasting offers is a new appreciation for whatever we deny ourselves. Food after hunger tastes sweeter and sharper, and satisfies more. And the excluded colors of the full spectrum, added back into a palette, shine with new vibrance and possibility.

Fasting, which on the surface seems to rob us of sensation, actually returns the world to us brighter. Our taste for it is improved by absence. Our understanding of it is deeper due to the loss.

For artists, who are deeply dependent on their own susceptibility to sensation, these effects can make fasting an invaluable tool, not just for clarifying vision, but reawakening senses dulled by work, noise, and worry.

Our poverty may be momentary or lifelong. It may be voluntary or the unintended consequence of a life in art.

But our willingness to face or endure poverty lays the foundation for all the other spiritual disciplines, by creating the freedom in which to practice them.

And poverty doesn't just release us from the pressures and distractions of the world.

It frees our hands to reach for the only true wealth: an encounter with God.

COMMUNITY

All of us are shaped by others.

We speak the language our parents spoke to us. We sing the songs we've heard and draw the faces we see. We're alive because someone else gave us years of food and shelter before we could earn or choose them. Even our fears and our confidence are often borrowed.

So all of us owe some great debt of gratitude, either to the people who first formed us, or to the people who helped set us free from the burden of that inheritance. Or, more likely, to both.

Some choices no one can make for us. Some responsibilities are ours alone, no matter how much we'd like to escape them. But our power to change ourselves is limited. We may struggle for years to root out one of our vices or release one of our virtues—and still fail.

But the effect others can have on us is profound. A stray word from a friend, a leader, a fellow artist—even an enemy—can give us new vision or confidence in a single instant, or save us years of wasted effort.

It can be humbling, and even infuriating, to discover that we are in no way our own architects. But that discovery alerts us to something most of us ignore: our great power to shape other lives, and the power of others to shape our own.

Life is full of attempts at control. Parents dictate rules to children. Children manipulate parents. Lovers and friends fight to change each other. Schools, businesses, religions, and governments invent programs to dominate entire societies.

These attempts may force us to adjust. But they operate against a deep internal resistance. And once the controls are removed, we often discover they never changed anything beyond the surface. Prison life may leave a prisoner afraid to go outside, but it does not heal her heart.

In contrast, the most transformative event in the lives of many people is becoming a parent. That transformation doesn't occur because of a child's ability to control anything, but because of the deep shifts that a child's total vulnerability provokes in a parent's life and heart.

And that same principle is at work, to some degree, in all human relationships. We are not transformed by powerful and ingenious attempts to control us, but when other people surrender their time, their heart, their story to us, not with an agenda or in any exchange, but with deep vulnerability, as a kind of gift.

Under these conditions, the smallest gesture can be explosively powerful. A small kindness can undo years of hurt. A teacher's stray comment can alter the course of a life. Other people can untie knots in us that we could never cut alone.

It is impossible to control others, and difficult to control ourselves. But when we recognize the power of community, we can make choices about who we want to be by choosing who we surrender to. When we create community, we create both ourselves and others.

So community itself may be one of the highest forms of art.

As Vincent van Gogh wrote: "there is nothing more truly artistic than to love people."

Historians of art are sometimes baffled by stories of great artists who somehow find their way to each other long before they achieve widespread fame. What are the odds that a tiny town in Alabama would produce both a Truman Capote and a Harper Lee, that a Patti Smith and a Robert Mapplethorpe would become best friends before either one became a household name, that Wes Anderson and Owen Wilson would both land in the same playwriting class at the same Texas university, that Diana Ross would grow up down the block from Smokey Robinson?

Maybe they simply connected because they were making the same moves. Smith and Mapplethorpe both moved to New York City to be part of the art world, and Anderson and Wilson both found their way into a playwriting class at a top school. But few of the other hopefuls who arrived in New York City or the University of Texas during those years have had anything like the impact of Mapplethorpe and Smith, or Anderson and Wilson.

Capote and Lee are an even more inexplicable pair: childhood friends who met in a rural town of three thousand and went on to become two of the best-read literary voices of their generation—and beyond.

Ross and Robinson, as kids, had never seen any Black singer rise to the stature and reach they both achieved. The fact that either of them became stars whose work is still foundational to world culture today is stunning. The fact that they grew up on the same street is so improbable that it wouldn't be believable as a plot point in a novel.

But none of these are episodes of blind luck. Instead, they're illustrations of the power of community: that no one might ever have heard of any of them, if they hadn't found each other.

On their own in Monroeville, at the University of Texas, or on the streets of New York or Detroit, they might easily have lost heart or lost their way.

Together, they not only survived, but created art that found a place in a much larger world.

And their strong bonds were just the beginning. Often, they formed the early links in even larger communities: film crews, New York's downtown scene, the Motown "family."

Community is distinct from movements, organizations, and cliques. The world is full of self-determined "in" and "out" groups that influence who receives attention and praise, and can help a career catch fire. But the deep transformative power that shapes an artist to welcome and act on inspiration is only released in the surrender of genuine community.

One of community's most basic functions is to teach. Community gives us tools we could spend a lifetime reinventing, and lessons we could waste a lifetime learning: the rule of thirds, the three-chord song, the three-act structure, how to hold a bow or fret a guitar. We might figure some of this out on our own, and we might reject some lessons a community tries to teach us. But we learn much faster together than alone.

In fact, all study can be seen as a variety of community, a way to interact with the minds that have gone before us, learn from them, and even count them among our friends.

Community doesn't just give us a foundation and a vocabulary. It gives us a laboratory to test what we learn.

And community gives us both courage and humility. The accomplishments of others challenge us, but at the same time, our own dreams expand. We can't believe what they achieved, or what they got away with.

But if they did, maybe we can, too.

Community reveals our identity, and strengthens it. Others see us in ways we can't, and help us hold on to who we are when we're in danger of forgetting. A community can help us keep creating, day after day, despite the world's deafening silence. And it can help us remember who we've always been, despite the deafening roar of success.

Community offers us energy when our own runs out. People who care about us can bang on our door, get us to the studio, ask when they're going to see the next pages, come up with the line we couldn't think of, and help us turn our impulses into habit, until habit wears a groove in our life that becomes a discipline that lasts even in solitude.

At its core, community is a cure for loneliness, which can drive us away from our instrument, canvas, or desk. It's possible to carry silence with us through the noise of the world, but we can also carry our community with us into solitude. Deep relationships are not extinguished by simple separation. So even in solitude, our community stands with us, invisible but still full of comfort and power.

Community doesn't just shape us as artists. Some of the world's best art can only be created in community: the great cathedrals, the movies, rock and roll.

In fact, when we look at the lives of artists who appear to be great loners, we see that virtually no one truly works alone. Even famous literary hermits like Emily Dickinson and Fernando Pessoa shared their work and found support in community, however small or secret.

An artist alone on a stage, or even a street corner, can sometimes create a moment more intense than any symphony or blockbuster. But when artists create together, the result can be orders of magnitude beyond what any of them could produce on their own.

When we welcome others into our art, it improves in two ways. First, a whole other mind is devoted to an area that we could only give a distracted glance. Instead of a drum machine, we have a living drummer, who not only has more skill than us, but brings a new stream of inspiration. At the same time, our own mind is no longer divided, so we can pour all our energy into our own strengths. Otis Redding doesn't have to play guitar—he's free to sing.

Community also activates an entire range of artists whose art can *only* emerge in collaboration: arrangers, costumers, great session players. To create, they need a composer, director, or band leader. But directors and composers also need them. No matter how brilliant his compositions, Bach could never have heard them, and neither could anyone else, if no one knew how to play a musical instrument. And a director's most vivid visions never translate to the stage or screen without the help of a small army of fellow artists.

In fact, the ability of a director, a conductor, or an architect to welcome others into a vision and orchestrate all the competing personalities and demands of a major production can be seen as a kind of artistic technique itself—and involve profound moments of inspiration.

The power of collaboration can only be released by humility: a recognition that what we need may lie beyond our own skill, power, or even perception. But the humility to ask for help also requires a profound confidence, not in ourselves, but in our vision: that it is worth enough to ask others to join us, to bring it into the world. And the friction of collaboration can also serve as a form of difficulty that refines the original vision, and welcomes new inspiration in everyone involved.

In any collaboration, clear vision is crucial. Everything from punk bands to high-budget films implode without it. Vision usually springs from an individual, and attempts to cast vision by committee almost always end in failure.

But to create together, we must share a vision. And the most effective directors, choreographers, and conductors don't seek to impose their inspiration as a rigid plan, but to light inspiration again in someone else.

The ways inspiration glows through each new artist, and the additional inspiration each artist brings, pose a real risk to the original vision. But they also offer enormous opportunity. Together, we can welcome far more inspiration than any one person could ever welcome alone.

If inspiration is an encounter with God, creating in community may be our only real hope to respond to it fully, because God is too vast to grasp with a single mind. To have any glimpse of the whole, we look together, with many minds.

Finally, no matter what kind of art we practice, our real work is never with sound or paper, motion or color.

Our art only lives when it lights again in another person.

So when we create community, and create in community, we work in our truest medium: the human heart and mind.

DISCERNMENT

Not every impulse is a good impulse.

Not every thought is a good thought.

Our mind absorbs all kinds of impressions, and our bodies produce all kinds of artifacts. We're often at war within ourselves. Our best impulses are deadlocked by worry. Our worst impulses are frighteningly powerful. Our hopes are weighed down by doubt. And our judgment, which could allow us to see through all this, is fragile: clouded by pride and fear, easily dethroned by the voices of others, swamped by passing emotions, or dulled by simple exhaustion.

Both art and the life of the spirit seek a voice that prompts us to act in ways that can run contrary to convention, and sometimes to reason. These impulses aren't just hard to explain, both to ourselves and others—often, they also demand profound risk and sacrifice.

And many people have more ideas for art than they could ever create in a single lifetime.

So how do we decide which impulses to follow?

For believers, discernment is a process of listening. They watch for an impulse they believe might come from God: spoken in their mind, by someone else, or through the world itself.

But they also compare those impulses to what they see as light from God in sacred texts, the wisdom of their community, their own experience, and the consequences of obedience, for themselves and others.

Art may not seem to offer an artist as much clear guidance. Some art scenes claim to have no rules, while some believers' lives seem to be full of them.

Believers may be tempted to overstate what they know. And artists may be tempted to overstate their ignorance. But the reality is that both artists and believers face similar uncertainty in seeking inspiration, or seeking God.

In fact, the possibilities for both the artist and the believer are endless. A believer may strictly obey commands to avoid murder, theft, greed, lies. But the positive commands of faith—to love our neighbor, serve others, follow the voice of God—contain infinite variations.

Both artists and believers also come in endless variety. So our impulses to create, or pray, or praise often take forms no one else has ever produced before.

This relentless originality is one of the hallmarks of both art and the presence of God. It also makes the task of discerning the voice of God from our own, or from other voices, more difficult, because we're not producing something uniform that can be tested against something else just like it.

But in both art and faith, our foundational act is to seek an encounter with something beyond ourselves: a spirit that guides our risks and sacrifices.

So both the believer and the artist ultimately return to the question of discernment: How do we recognize the voice of inspiration, or the voice of God?

How do we discern true encounters with a spirit beyond ourselves from our own fears or passing thoughts, or from the noise and echoes of the world?

Artists do have a form of scripture. Although canons are contested, we can compare our work with whatever we believe is true art. Learning to recognize inspiration in the work of others can help us recognize inspiration when it speaks in us.

Community, with our fellow artists or with others, can offer wisdom and perspective, helping us to sort what's genuinely inspired from our own pride, fear, and false starts.

Time also tests inspiration. It burns away both the believer's false fervor and the artist's vanity or ambition. And it stills the confusion of contemporary praise or derision. A remove of several days, or many years, can make what is and is not inspired in our work starkly, even painfully, clear.

Humility is a crucial element in discernment. With humility, we know our weaknesses. But humility also recognizes that we did not choose, or even earn, most of our strengths. The artist's eye, the singer's voice, the pianist's hands, the author's memory, the actor's grace: all of these are accidents of birth or luck, as are most of the experiences that shape us, for better or worse.

So genuine humility gives birth to gratitude, and gratitude—the recognition of how much we have that we did not earn—can build humility. Both of them remind us how little we have, and how little we can do, by ourselves. And letting that truth sink in deep can make us even more receptive—to the world, to what others have to offer, and to inspiration.

Humility is also a practical requirement in creation. Inspiration prompts us to create, but every gesture we make is not inspired. Sometimes inspiration arrives with almost painful clarity. More often it seems faint and fitful. We strain to hear it in hints and snatches, and we capture it in any form we can.

Then we begin to sort and assemble: to cut the rock from diamond and set the gem—or to nurture and teach the new child. We still find inspiration in this process. But it also requires humility, because so often what we need to remove is our own thoughts, plans, habits, and prejudices, in order to reveal what is most alien to us: the artifacts of genuine inspiration.

To refine our work, we surrender to it, as the first member of our own audience. Other people may have a cooler mind to examine our work. They can tell us how successfully our vision translated to them, and teach us things we could never learn by relying on our single mind.

But only we can measure our work against our original inspiration. Nobody else saw or heard what we did, so nobody else can do that for us. If they could, we wouldn't have an original voice as an artist.

Where our work fails to match our inspiration, we wait to discover more, or we cut. Sometimes those cuts trim back the underbrush to reveal a true form that had been obscured by our false starts or excesses. Sometimes, when we clear away the rubble of our own thoughts and false starts, we find nothing left.

To leave that space open for the real action of inspiration, instead of filling it again with whatever we have at hand, is an act of humility.

It's also an act of hope.

The paradox of true humility is that it can only flow from a confidence so deep it might better be described as faith. It's not confidence in ourselves. We see our own weaknesses all too clearly. Instead, we have confidence because we know we draw on something else.

We dare to create because we believe inspiration will lead us beyond what we could do alone. We can cut away our failures because we believe that inspiration will arrive to take their place.

This kind of humility requires a constant reckoning with our weaknesses.

But it is not weakness.

It takes enormous courage, and it shows enormous courage, to face the truth about our limits.

It takes even more courage to refuse to accept those truths as final: to reach past them, into something beyond our understanding or control, for something better than ourselves.

In the end, a mystic does not recognize God, and an artist does not recognize inspiration, by any set of procedures or laws.

Both art and faith attempt to meet something that complicates and transcends all laws. So our attempts to discern the voice of God, or inspiration, will never be perfectly rational. They may never be replicable. They may not even be accurate.

We can never know for certain that we've heard the voice of God, or inspiration.

But sometimes we know it, without question, at our core.

We know it the same way we recognize any other voice. Very few of us could give a description clear enough to help someone else recognize the voice of our mother or father. But because we know them so well—both the kind of things they say and the sound of their voices—we recognize them in an instant. And we know in an instant when a voice is not theirs as well.

The voice of inspiration is the same way: clear and indescribable. We discern it best by simple familiarity, the way government agents learn to recognize counterfeit cash: not by studying fakes, but the real thing.

Or the way we know our own way home: not by rote, but by heart.

We can't identify inspiration with charts or point to it on maps. But we learn to recognize it when we have the courage to act on what we know, despite the fact that we may never prove it: the action that lies at the heart of all faith, and all art.

OBEDIENCE

The spiritual life, and the life of the artist, don't just require the skill to listen and know, but courage and strength to act.

We do not still ourselves in order to end all action, in a kind of premature death. We listen, at least in part, for the shape of our next act.

In much of the world, obedience has a bad name. "Obedient" is only a compliment to a child or a pet, not a grown person.

But even in a child, obedience requires strength, to do what we're asked, not just what we want. As adults, that strength blossoms into command of ourselves. And the stubborn will to obey our own conscience or vision, despite the commands or threats of others, is the seed of all revolution.

Art arrives from something better and wiser than us, stranger and more complete. We are not capable of compassing it, because it is greater than us. And if we insist on a full explanation before we act, it will slip through our hands. We can only welcome it by obedience, no matter how inconvenient, ridiculous, or terrifying.

In the presence of knowledge beyond our understanding, obedience is only sanity: the obedience of a patient to a doctor, a builder to an engineer, a student to a teacher.

This obedience can take any form, from forcing ourselves to record a note instead of falling back to sleep, to staking our entire reputation on a project we have no idea how to complete.

It introduces us to ourselves in new ways, turning us away from the familiar paths we tread or wounds we probe, to the ones we can't even stand to name: not the lover who betrayed us, but the mother who did; not our regrets, but our cowardice; not our fear of love, but the fact we'd kill for it.

But the same light that invades our darkest corners also leads us down new paths. Our own will, unbridled, rarely takes us anywhere new. Even or perhaps especially in our fiercest tantrums, our impulses are mired in habit and our minds spin in familiar circles. We don't break free of these traps by pitting our own will against itself, which only divides or paralyzes us.

But as we follow inspiration, we discover a beautiful paradox: that to obey it has become our own deepest desire. Our longing to answer its voice is not a duty, but an ache, a hope, and a joy.

And as we obey inspiration, it leads us to places we would never find on our own, both within and beyond ourselves.

SERVICE

The work that the spirit accomplishes in us in through the spiritual disciplines doesn't have to explain itself, to earn anything, or even to be seen, in order to have great value.

But the strength we develop and the visions that come to us, all we learn and all we create, are not just for ourselves.

Artists throughout history have been among the first to respond to the needs around us, perhaps because our work requires us to stay sensitive to everything, including hardship others glance past. Van Gogh was criticized, while working for a church, for giving up his own lodging to a homeless man. Tolstoy famously warred with his wife because he wanted to give away huge chunks of his inherited wealth.

The sensitivity of artists to the suffering of others, and to their own consciences, has also set them at the forefront of movements for social change across the world. American actors and singers marched alongside civil rights leaders at the 1963 March on Washington. Chinese art students created the Goddess of Liberty statue at Tiannamen Square. Thomas Mapfumo's music was so central to the Zimbabwean fight for independence that government forces blasted it from helicopters, hoping to discourage rebels by making them think Mapfumo himself had stopped supporting them—a tactic that never worked.

The general public may think of art as an afterthought or a distraction, but repressive governments never make this mistake. They're quick to employ the arts to create propaganda. And they're even quicker to squash dissenting voices among artists—precisely because those governments recognize the power of art.

At moments of crisis and change, the world turns to artists.

But we need to serve at least as much as the world needs us.

Acts of service can put us in touch with people we might never otherwise know, introducing us to new worlds, new ways of seeing, singing, speaking. Service can connect us with communities that support us in ways we could never guess. And it can give us the blessing of manual labor: concrete tasks that we know are done when we finish them—unlike our art, which we can work on for days or years without being certain we're on the right path, or that we'll ever reach the end of it.

A path we're not sure we see, with an end we may never reach: this can describe our art, but it also describes true service. No attempt to serve comes with a guarantee. And the places with the most need often pose the highest risk of hardship and failure. So our tolerance for uncertainty as artists builds our strength to serve. And the uncertainty we feel as we serve builds strength to face it as we create.

Art is not a substitute for service. None of us serve the world so well through our art that we don't need to get our hands dirty or our hearts broken by more direct confrontations with trouble and need.

But creating art is an act of service, even when we don't know who it will help, or how.

It's impossible to know who our art will ultimately reach.

But all of us have been touched by artists whose work has persisted long beyond their own time, changing the lives of people they couldn't imagine would ever see it.

Seeing our art as an act of service can change the way we create. Creation is no longer about self-indulgence or self-expression, because what we create is not just for us. And it's not just for an audience, to dazzle, entertain, or build our fame.

Instead, we hope that in some way our work will be a gift or a light, sustenance, shelter, or balm.

Art can do all this, and more. But it is also a good in itself, in ways that we can't name or plan, and in ways that constantly shift. And that fundamental, inexpressible good can be ruined, or quickly turned to propaganda, if we insist we know exactly how it must serve.

Recognizing creation as service can give us both freedom and strength. It can unwind paralyzing perfectionism. If we have water and someone is thirsty in the desert, we don't need the world's best glass or garnish. We just need to share what we've got.

But seeing our art as service also raises the stakes. We're not just trying to decorate or entertain. If our art might actually serve someone, might meet some deep need, it deserves everything we have to give.

When we believe we work only for ourselves, whether we do it on a grand stage or have no stage at all, it's easy for us to treat our art in the same mixed-up ways we often treat ourselves: to forget or neglect or even starve it, to place everything else ahead of it, to put unbearable pressure on it—or to pamper it in all the wrong ways.

But when we see our art as an act of service, we can give not just what we would give to ourselves, but what we'd give to someone else.

As we create, we can become more generous, with our art and with ourselves.

And that can create profound shifts in what comes to us, and what comes through us, into the world.

DISCIPLINE AND INSPIRATION

The spiritual disciplines are not techniques, tactics, or hacks: they're practices with the power to transform our whole lives.

And their power is unlocked, not when we learn a trick or a secret, but by rhythm and by time.

Each of these disciplines has something to offer everyone, but no discipline will look the same for all of us. Even if we could perfectly replicate the patterns of our heroes, they wouldn't resonate the same way in our own lives. And rigidly reproducing their patterns won't help us to produce art like theirs—or our own.

Instead, different disciplines will work in different ways for each of us, in different seasons. That's why they've persisted through time, and still matter now.

So as we step into the spiritual disciplines, each of us will invent our own process. Some of us may start with what we're most drawn to. Some of us may start with what we fear most. Some of us may lean into a single discipline for a long season. Some of us may cycle between several, or begin with one and build in discipline after discipline.

The way we welcome the spiritual disciplines into our lives may even be a place where inspiration itself meets and guides us.

The power of the spiritual disciplines is never in perfection, but in practice. Our false starts, our bursts of enthusiasm, our confusion, our fitful patterns—the spiritual disciplines are wide and deep enough, old and strong enough, to compass them all.

There's great power in our patterns of life, in doing the same thing each day, each time, and recognizing by that how much we or the world have changed, how far we've gotten, how much we've created.

And there's value in doing things whether we feel like it or not, in showing up to listen for inspiration even when it feels absolutely distant from us.

But the goal of the disciplines is never simply to keep an appointment, or even a promise.

The goal is not to pray each day at the same time. It's prayer that never ends.

We may start anywhere—even with rest.

We may fall down, give up, get lost.

Rest or work, gratitude or prayer, may look very different for us than it does for anyone else.

But if we continue to return to the disciplines, we will find inspiration leading us deeper into each of them.

And in every discipline, we'll find more inspiration, in both our art, and our lives.

THE DISCIPLINE OF ART

All spiritual disciplines can form and strengthen us as artists.
But the creation of art is also a spiritual discipline.
Our acts of creation don't just form us to welcome inspiration, but to welcome God.
An opera singer who listens to her own voice as she trains also tunes herself to listen for the voice of God.
An actor who builds the mental strength to surrender to the momentum of a story also builds the mental strength to surrender to God.
The practice of art forms us as spiritual beings, because the artist's search to find and know the living spirit of creation and the seeker's search to find and know God are, at heart, the same act.
To come to our art with strong hands and a clear mind doesn't just require one corner of our life. It requires our whole lives.
The demands of creation reveal strengths and weaknesses in us that we may even have attempted to hide from ourselves.
And as we confront our hidden possibilities and pain again and again in the act of creation, our whole lives can be transformed.

To understand art as a spiritual discipline answers another question: If God gives the seed of art in inspiration, why must it come through an artist?

Why does it take so much trouble and time, so much risk and failure?

Why do so many visions end in disappointment?

Why is so much only half-seen, or half-formed?

Why does art not come into the world whole and perfect, direct from God?

Or at least spring fully formed from us?

But if art is a spiritual discipline, its primary goal is not the creation of artifacts.

It is our encounter with God.

And the primary artifact of that encounter is not the product of our hands.

It is the artist ourselves.

God's interest, and even insistence, on creating through our imperfection and brokenness is a sign of God's love for us.

God is less concerned with the creation of art than the creation of the artist.

Art is evidence of God's presence.

But the purpose of God's presence in inspiration is not to create art.

It is to create us.

As van Gogh wrote in a letter to a friend, Christ "lived serenely as an artist greater than all artists—disdaining marble and clay and paint—working in LIVING FLESH. . . . This extraordinary artist, hardly conceivable with the obtuse instrument of our nervous and stupefied modern brains, made neither statues nor paintings nor even books . . . he states it loud and clear . . . he made LIVING men, immortals."

Van Gogh sees the creation of humankind as a masterpiece of God.

But God did not leave creation behind when it was complete.

God is still present, and still creating: both the world, and each of us.

So art is not only a tool we use to shape the perishable world.

It is a tool God uses to shape the imperishable in all of us.

CONCLUSIONS

EVERYONE IS AN ARTIST, EVERYTHING IS ART

To understand art as evidence of the presence of God upends traditional notions of what is and isn't art.

And it explodes our traditional categories of who is and who is not an artist.

If art's defining characteristic is the surrender to inspiration, then any person can welcome that voice.

Art is not the special property of some special breed called "artist."

Inspiration is present in all lives.

Anyone who surrenders to it can be an artist.

And anything in the world can be art.

Some part of us already knows this. Our basic necessities of food, clothing, and shelter, in the right hands, are also seen as art: cuisine, fashion, architecture. And when we see an inspired performance of anything from walking a tightrope, to bricklaying, to barbecue, we say they've "got it down to an art." Or, "they're an artist."

But inspiration doesn't just emerge in what we think of as the arts.

Alexander Pushkin, the great Russian poet, wrote that "inspiration is needed in geometry as much as poetry." His opinion, as a poet, might be suspect. But it's echoed by everyone from sports stars, who know that conscious control can make them clutch, to scientists themselves.

The solution to the problem of how to thread the needle of the original sewing machine came to Isaac Singer in a dream. Russian chemist Dmitri Mendeleev recorded seeing the periodic table of elements for the first time in a dream, and mathematician Srinivasa Ramanujan, whose theorems we are only now beginning to comprehend a century after his death, claimed a goddess gave him solutions in his sleep as well. "An equation for me has no meaning," he wrote, "unless it represents a thought of God."

All of us create something that could be defined as art, even if it's simply dinner or a choice about what to wear the next day. Almost everyone, at some point in our lives, has scrawled down a poem, whistled or sung, drawn a picture, or broken into dance.

Businesspeople often describe the moment when they get to "be creative" as their favorite part of their job. We even punish people by denying their creative impulses: the way every sign of human individuality is erased in the uniformity of a prison. And the birth and nurture of children—the focus of most human life—is more creative, and carries more consequences, than most of us can bear to admit.

When people are set free from the demands and distractions of the world, we often begin to produce art—even if we never claimed the name of artist before. Prisoners fill pages with poetry and create tapestries with thread pulled from the colored stripes of socks. Becalmed sailors embroidered "woolies" depicting distant shores, exotic creatures, and their own ships, or filled shadow boxes with intricate patterns in tiny shells to make "sailor's valentines." Presidents and prime ministers retire, and begin to paint. Late in life, the residents of rest homes often begin for the first time to draw and write, or even dance and sing. At opposite ends of the economic spectrum, both poor and rich spend free moments in creation, whether that takes the form of graffiti or growing orchids.

Brain damage and neurological disease can also prompt artistic expression from people who never showed any previous interest, or received any previous training, in art. And the art that they produce is often remarkable.

But it doesn't take injury to the brain to reveal the prevalence of inspiration. People talk frequently about ideas for movies we will never make or books we will never write, sometimes imagined with enormous care and detail. Some of us even hear music, especially when waking or falling asleep, that we know we've never heard, and have no ability to recapture or translate.

But perhaps the best proof of the presence of inspiration in all people is a child. All children dance, sing, and draw. Every child knows that she can do these things. But before we leave elementary school, most of us begin to believe that we "can't."

As Picasso observed: every child has a genius for art. But as we grow up, it often seems to vanish.

Not everyone who sings needs to do it in an amphitheater. And not everyone who tells a story should command the attention of the world.

But in the industrialized West, we have learned this lesson with an almost tragic thoroughness. We believe art is only valid when it attracts an audience, preferably a large and paying one. Without an audience, we often hesitate to call ourselves artists, even if we've devoted years to our art.

But commercial traction is a famously unreliable measure of artistic success, especially in an artist's own time. Artists sell millions of copies of work that no one can remember the title of a decade later. But Herman Melville could not support himself as an author for much of his life. Vincent van Gogh only sold one painting in his. The vast majority of Fernando Pessoa's work was unpublished, packed in a trunk at the time of his death, although he is now considered one of Portugal's greatest authors. The year Bach premiered his *St. Matthew Passion*, most local residents of Leipzig went to see a competing production by a composer who was considered more promising. While she lived, Emily Dickinson never had more than a handful of readers outside her own family, and Walt Whitman's *Leaves of Grass* sold a small fraction of the volumes sold by his contemporary Longfellow, who is virtually unread today.

And artists do not ever have to achieve fame in order for our work to matter. An audience does not have to fill an amphitheater or push a book up the bestseller lists for the connection between an artist and an audience to be deep and transformative. And amphitheaters and bestsellers do not always offer the most satisfying experience for audiences, or the best home for artists.

In fact, the parent or lover who sings a lullaby to an audience of one may give a far more important performance than a star who sings to thousands. A star may have unique talent and power. But if they leave the stage, another star will emerge on that same stage. If a parent or lover does not sing, there is no other to sing in our place.

Often, when people are confronted with art, our creative impulses emerge in the form of a protest: "I could never do that."

But those objections reveal an underlying sense of call.

Art doesn't show us what we aren't, but what we all could be.

It doesn't promise us that we can all sing like Aretha Franklin. But it reminds us that we all have voices to sing.

All our self-doubt and pride are thrown into absurd relief by comparison with a single bird. She doesn't sing for money or fame, because she believes she sings better than other birds, or even to express herself. Instead, she sings in obedience to her own architecture. She may sing for any number of reasons: to bless or scold the morning, to mourn a loss, call a lover, send a warning. But at the most fundamental level, she sings because she is a bird.

It's clear that the world needs both Mavis Staples's and Aretha Franklin's versions of "Amazing Grace." But it's also possible that the world needs the version of "Amazing Grace" sung by every voice, no matter how small, magnificent, or broken. The most moving moment of a concert doesn't happen when a singer, no matter how talented, stands alone on stage, but when the entire audience joins in.

That sound actually constitutes its own voice—and may be an echo of the voice of God.

Inspiration speaks in all of us, but it rarely results in art. That fact has given inspiration a bad name.

But we could also consider the enormous amount of inspiration that never comes to fruition as a tragedy, a loss of epic proportions.

We would consider it a crime against humanity if someone burned the Motown master tapes, or smashed every Rodin. The loss of the books in the library at Alexandria still echoes through history thousands of years later.

But exponentially more art has been lost to us simply because it was never made.

Inspiration may go unanswered for many reasons: because someone who didn't believe he was an artist was too fearful to respond, because someone known as an artist chose to do something less demanding and easier to understand, because the person who received the inspiration lived in bondage that made it impossible to act on her inspiration.

The fact that so many people through history, and today, have lived under conditions that made it very difficult to create should give those of us who are only scared some motivation, from gratitude that we have the opportunity.

But reckoning with the enormous amount of inspiration that has been lost to us can come with great hope: the recognition of how much art still waits to break into the world, in all places, through all people.

That hope encourages us to see, and seek, art everywhere.

And to look for the artist, burning bright or buried, in everyone we meet—including ourselves.

The creative force of God is not held captive in the moment of artistic inspiration.

It can author and illuminate our whole lives.

And we need the strengths that welcome inspiration not just to create, but to live: the courage to listen and express, wait and risk, for unspeakable reasons and uncertain rewards.

We don't surrender to inspiration because we are good at it, but because it is good for us.

And when we do, we can welcome inspiration into every part of our lives—and any part of our lives can be transformed by inspiration, into art.

THE GREAT ARTIST

Art provokes enormous curiosity about the artist.

We want to know who they are, how they did what they did, what they think it all means.

But even as we sort through an artist's interviews and paint ingredients, looking for the recipe for the sublime, we have a sense of our own ridiculousness.

And the more we learn about any artist, the more we find ourselves among ashes and shadows, disappointed or betrayed.

The longing art provokes in us can never be satisfied by any artist, because that longing is not for the artist, but for God.

And the understanding that art comes from God introduces us to the true object of our worship, and the only thing that can withstand it.

Our hunger for art, our joy in movement, sound, beauty, taste, touch: none of these things can finally fill or transform us.

But at the same time, we know that they are not empty or false.

All the beauty and promise that ever betrayed us or couldn't bear the weight of our need: it all shows us a glimpse of God.

Every face echoes God's face.

All beauty both reveals and leads us back to God.

To say that God prompts art, and that God is present in art, is not to say that art is God. That would be like pointing to a human artist's work and claiming that it was, in fact, the artist.

But art does reveal something about an artist.

And because art flows from God, it offers clues to God.

Like God, art has an eternal signature that is expressed with endless variation.

Like God, art prompts more art—the surest sign of whether a seed is alive or not.

And art begins to fail when it is not like God: when it is repetitive instead of generous, when it substitutes any lie for truth.

Art also hints at God's delight, both in the act of creation, and in created things.

God could easily continue God's performance at the dawn of time, speaking new things into being out of nothing.

But by calling new things into the world through human hands, minds, and voices, God seems fiercely committed to the original creation: to every individual, to the smallest details, each of our hidden or lonely acts, the wild variety of time and place.

Art can be seen as God pointing to both the original creation, and the world around us now, and reminding us, as at the beginning, that "it is good."

God can also be seen as an artist who makes their own materials: a painter who mixes his own pigments, a musician who builds her own guitar.

Every artist presents God with new opportunities.

And rather than discarding us due to our imperfections, God seems to take special joy in refracting new light through the broken glass of our hearts, and lives, and world.

Our longing to create is a longing to meet God.

So is the longing that draws us back to a favorite painting, to the dance club, to the movies, to a song.

Art is transcendent because it marks a place where God has been, and because it is a place where we meet God.

But God is not a muse, who only has the power to animate flesh, paper, and greasepaint.

The restless energy of all music also set the world in motion.

The organizing principle of all poems also organized the stars.

And God is able to transform our lives and hearts with the same force and beauty we find in the creation of the world, and the creation of art.

As we seek God, both as inspiration and in life, we should never accept a faith that cannot offer us everything art does, that does not unwind and comfort, sear and revive us like art, that is not as vivid, incalculable, demanding, beautiful, and wise.

And when we find these elements in art, we can recognize them as the evidence and the home of a true meeting with God.

NOTES

9 **"giftless bastard"** Pyotr Ilyich Tchaikovsky, diary entry for October 9, 1886, quoted in Nicolas Slonimsky, *Lexicon of Musical Invective* (New York: Norton, 1953), 73.

9 **"be anything but a dauber"** Annah de Pui Miller, *"Who and What": A Compendium of General Information* (Philadelphia: Lippincott, 1878), 401.

9 **"should have stuck to flying machines"** In Bill Swainson, ed., *Encarta Book of Quotations* (New York: St. Martin's Press, 2000), 558.

10 **"a catastrophe of awkwardness"** Colin Jarman, *The Book of Poisonous Quotes* (New York: McGraw-Hill Education, 1993), 40.

10 **compares Mondrian to a fart** Steven D. Price, *The Most Low-Down, Lousiest, Loathsome Things Ever Said* (Essex, CT: Lyons, 2017), 253.

10 **"out-uglying"** Salvador Dalí, *Dalí on Modern Art: The Cuckolds of Antiquated Modern Art*, trans. Haakon M. Chevalier (Mineola, NY: Dover, 1996), 21.

10 **"a queasy undergraduate scratching his pimples"** Virginia Woolf, diary entry August 16, 1922, quoted in Emily Temple, "A Selection of Virginia Woolf's Most Savage Insults," *Literary Hub*, October 12, 2017.

10 **Frida Kahlo says she'd rather sit on the floor** Frida Kahlo, letter to Nickolas Muray, February 16, 1939, Nickolas Muray Papers, 1910–1992. Archives of American Art, Smithsonian Institution.

10 *the purpose of art is to conceal the artist*   Oscar Wilde, *The Picture of Dorian Gray* (New York: Brentanos, 1913), xiii.

10 *an artist's self is all they have to sell*   Matthew J. Bruccoli, ed., *F. Scott Fitzgerald: A Life in Letters* (New York: Simon & Schuster, 1995), 368.

10 *art requires much calm*   Fra Angelico, quoted in Jacques Maritain, *Art and Scholasticism*, chapter 8, https://tinyurl.com/yffpbxuh.

10 *reads the newspaper "with fury."*   Vincent van Gogh to his sister Wil, quoted in Martin Gayford, *The Yellow House* (Boston: Mariner Books, 2008), 76.

10 *"there is no method but to be very intelligent"*   T. S. Eliot, "The Perfect Critic," https://tinyurl.com/bdefvhxx.

10 *poetry has little to do with intelligence*   Jorge Luis Borges, "The Art of Fiction," interview with Roland Christ (1967), in *The Paris Review Interviews*, vol. 1 (New York: Picador, 2006), 138.

10 *the vastest intelligence cannot bring art about*   James McNeill Whistler, *Mister Whistler's "Ten O'Clock"* (Boston: Houghton Mifflin, 1888), 21.

15 *"Tell me the story, muse"*   Homer, *The Odyssey*, trans. E. V. Rieu, rev. D. C. H. Rieu (London: Penguin, 2003), 3.

15 *"You don't write melodies, you find them"*   "Hoagy Concert at Murat Big Success," *Indianapolis Sunday Star*, quoted in Richard M. Sudhalter, *Stardust Melody: The Life and Music of Hoagy Carmichael* (Oxford: Oxford University Press, 2003), 84.

16 *"There is no theory. You only have to listen"*   Richard Taruskin, *Music in the Early Twentieth Century: The Oxford History of Western Music* (Oxford: Oxford University Press, 2006), 70.

16 *"I hear it, and my hand's too slow"*   "Clemente x 8, Featuring Francesco Clemente and Nas," September 4, 2014, The Rubin Museum, New York City, from author's notes.

16 *"I saw the angel in the marble"*   Michelangelo Buonarotti, quoted in Anthony Blunt, *Artistic Theory in Italy* (Oxford: Oxford University Press, 1962), 73.

16   *Dante, in his Divine Comedy*   Dante Alighieri, *The Divine Comedy: Purgatorio*, 24.45–54, trans. Jean Hollander and Robert Hollander (Albany: Anchor, 2004), 531.

16   *"I don't think a writer should meddle"*   Jorge Luis Borges, "The Art of Fiction," interview with Roland Christ (1967), in *Paris Review Interviews*, 1:131.

16   *"The song will ultimately tell me what it wants"*   Lamont Dozier and Scott B. Bomar, *How Sweet It Is: A Songwriter's Reflections on Music, Motown, and the Mysteries of the Muse* (New York: BMG Books, 2019), 268, 8.

16   *"Most of the time, it seemed"*   Patti Smith, *Just Kids* (London: Bloomsbury, 2019), 56.

16   *Sam Cooke describes a similar experience*   "Sam Cooke and the Song That 'Almost Scared Him,'" *All Things Considered*, NPR, February 1, 2014.

16   *"The song just came to me"*   Quoted in Peter Guralnik, *Dream Boogie: The Triumph of Sam Cooke* (New York: Back Bay Books, 2006), 540.

17   *"The song wrote itself"*   Quoted in Paul Zollo, *Songwriters on Songwriting*, exp. 4th ed. (Boston: Da Capo, 2003), 143.

17   *"being open—not scratching for it"*   Toni Morrison, quoted in Pam Houston, "Toni Morrison: The Precious Moments a Writer Lives For," in *Oprah Magazine*, July 2009.

17   *"Thomas looked into himself"*   Sherman Alexie, *Reservation Blues* (New York: Grove, 2005), 167.

17   *"real shock . . . I didn't write this"*   Peggy Whitman Prenshaw, ed., *Conversations with Eudora Welty* (Jackson: University Press of Mississippi, 1998), 76.

17   *"If a writer is any good"*   Flannery O'Connor, *The Nature and Aim of Fiction* (New York: Farrar, Straus and Giroux, 1979), 83.

17   *"When I read it I would think this is so good"*   Ernest Hemingway, "The Strange Country," in *The Complete Short Stories of Ernest Hemingway*, Finca Vigia Edition (New York: Scribner, 2007), 645.

17 **"I'm interested in what I find"**   Quoted in Zollo, *Songwriters on Songwriting*, 95.

18 **"Neither this work nor those to follow"**   Fernando Pessoa, *The Selected Prose of Fernando Pessoa*, trans. Richard Zenith (New York: Grove, 2001), 2.

18 *something in her knew how to write poetry*   Quoted in Kamilah Aisha Moon, "Visitation: A Poet's Gathering," *Mentor and Muse: Essays from Poets to Poets*, https://tinyurl.com/mn6589az.

18 **"I readily acknowledge"**   Kamilah Aisha Moon, "Watching a Woman on the M101 Express," *New American Poets*, Poetry Society of America, https://tinyurl.com/yeyrjxb9.

18 **"It's like a blackout"**   Beyonce Knowles, quoted in Amy Wallace, "Miss Millennium: Beyonce," *GQ*, January 10, 2013.

18 **"I have written the poems from immediate dictation"**   William Blake, "Letter of 25 April 1803," quoted in Edward Bliss Reed, *English Lyrical Poetry from Its Origins to the Present Time* (New Haven: Yale University Press, 1912), 380.

18 **"I didn't want to write it"**   Quoted in Dave Thompson, *1000 Songs That Rock Your World* (Iola, WI: Krause, 2011), 243.

18 **"If I exhaust my will enough"**   Marie Howe, at Rubin Museum Lunch Conversations, October 15, 2013, author's notes.

19 **"pessimistic, nihilistic actions and assertions"**   Gerhard Richter, "July 25, 1989," in *Gerhard Richter: Writings* (New York: Distributed Art Publishers, 2009), 213.

19 **"creating or discovering hope"**   *Gerhard Richter: October Files 8*, ed. Benjamin H. D. Buchloh (Cambridge: MIT Press, 1986), 24.

19 **"Excuse me, can you not see that I'm driving?"**   Quoted in Kim Zetter, "*Eat, Pray, Love* Author on How We Kill Geniuses," February 6, 2009, https://tinyurl.com/4xdcjv67.

19 **"Songwriting is like fishing in a stream"**   Quoted in Paul Zollo, "Bob Dylan: The Interview, Part 1," https://tinyurl.com/96a4hkdt.

19 *"Carry a pen at all times"* Anne Lamott, Facebook post, April 3, 2013, https://tinyurl.com/4fud37y6.

19 *"I can't," Jackson answered* Quoted in Claire Hoffman, "The Last Days of Michael Jackson," *Rolling Stone*, August 6, 2009.

20 *"We carry thousands of years of . . . blood and memory"* Martha Graham, *Blood Memory: An Autobiography* (New York: Doubleday, 1991), 10.

20 *"Unless you believe that someone is sending you a signal"* Quoted in Zollo, *Songwriters on Songwriting*, 120.

20 *"No longer do I believe that there is a mystic muse"* Wallace Stevens, *The Necessary Angel: Essays on Reality and the Imagination* (New York: Knopf Doubleday, 2011), 60.

22 *"I dislike learned talk about 'the unconscious,'"* Wendell Berry, *Imagination in Place* (Berkeley: Counterpoint, 2010), 6.

22 *"We ain't even really rapping"* Tupac Shakur, "1994 Swedish P3 Radio Interview," sampled on "Mortal Man" by Kendrick Lamar, *To Pimp a Butterfly* (Aftermath/Interscope, 2015).

22 *"rock 'n' roll was so strange that it had to come from Mars"* Quoted in Griel Marcus, *Mystery Train* (New York: Plume, 1997), 143.

23 *Brian Wilson, Carole King, Burt Bacharach, and Lamont Dozier* Zollo, *Songwriters on Songwriting*, 128, 137, 212; Dozier and Bomar, *How Sweet It Is*, 9.

23 *"I believe that He's the author of all this stuff"* Quoted in Zollo, *Songwriters on Songwriting*, 166.

23 *"wasn't done by me, Smoke"* Smokey Robinson and David Ritz, *Inside My Life* (New York: McGraw Hill, 1989), 160.

23 *Robinson himself described his own songwriting* Kiah Welsh, "5 Motown Classics You Didn't Know Smokey Robinson Wrote," *CBC Music*, February 7, 2017.

23 *"the gift that God gave me"* Quoted in J. D. Heyman, Tom Gliatto, and Melody Chiu, "Farewell to the Queen of Soul," *People* 90, no. 11 (September 3, 2018): 58.

23 *"It was as if the Lord said"* Quoted in Lydia Hutchinson, "Oz Anniversary: Behind 'Somewhere Over the Rainbow,'" November 3, 2014, https://tinyurl.com/3rxjwvh2.

23 *"Ideas reside in the same place as prayers"* Quoted in Rob Shepherd, "Sound Is Everywhere: A Conversation with Jeff Coffin (Part Two)," *Post Genre: Music Beyond Category*, September 10, 2022.

23 *"This is what God has created me to be"* Quoted in Brian Marks, "DMX's Ex-Wife Tashera Simmons Shares His Final Words to Her One Week before His Death: 'My Voice Will Be Stronger When I'm Gone,'" May 17, 2021, https://tinyurl.com/yrnc22rp.

23 *"as an offering to God"* Rick Rubin, "Superwolves: Bonnie 'Prince' Billy and Matt Sweeney," *Broken Record* podcast, May 18, 2021.

23 *"I wrote at Thy command"* Rainer Maria Rilke, *Where Silence Reigns* (New York: New Directions, 1978), 147.

23 *It's an echo of poet Elizabeth Barrett Browning* Elizabeth Barrett Browning, "Aurora Leigh," quoted in Lyndal Gordon, *Lives Like Loaded Guns: Emily Dickinson and Her Family's Feuds* (New York: Penguin, 2011), 84.

23 *"I had a kind of feeling"* Anne Sexton, "The Art of Poetry No. 15," interview by Barbara Kevles, in *Writers at Work: The Paris Review Interviews* (New York: Viking, 1976), 418.

24 *"I am not painting"* Werner Herzog, *Cave of Forgotten Dreams* (film, Revolver Entertainment, 2011).

24 *"God held my hand"* Henri Matisse, Marie-Alain Couturier, and Louise-Bertrand Rayssiguier, *The Vence Chapel: Archive of a Creation* (Milan: Skira Editoire, 1999), 303.

24 *"It's much like the life of a Catholic nun"* Quoted in Zollo, *Songwriters on Songwriting*, 335.

24 *"Carole says they come from God"* Quoted in Spencer Leigh, "Gerry Goffin: Prolific Songwriter Whose Work with His Wife Carole King Helped Shape the Course of Popular Music," *The Independent*, June 20, 2014.

24 *"Where they come from"*   Quoted in Zollo, *Songwriters on Songwriting*, 212.

36 *Victor Hugo engaged in hundreds of conversations*   Victor Hugo, *Les Misérables*, ed. Laurence M. Porter (New York: Barnes and Noble Classics, 2003), 5–6.

36 *And the legend of bluesman Robert Johnson*   Mack McCormick, *Biography of a Phantom* (New York: Penguin, 2023), 161–62.

42 *"I believe in God, man"*   *Freaks and Geeks*, season 1, episode 1, "Pilot." Directed by Jake Kasdan. Aired September 25, 1999, on NBC.

44 *the New York Public Library*   "Splendour among Shadows," New York Public Library, September 8–28, 2016.

53 *"It doesn't care what you are doing"*   Quoted in Mark Richard, "The Music of Chance," *Spin Magazine (USA)*, June 1994, 101.

61 *"A man's life is interwoven into his music"*   Quoted in Stephen Braun, "Legends Nureyev, Gillespie Die: Jazz Trumpeter Sparked Be-Bop Revolution," *Los Angeles Times*, January 7, 1993.

61 *"you have to be there"*   Alex Dueben, "Words Can Sustain and Save Us: *The Millions* Interviews Marie Howe," *The Millions*, January 11, 2018.

61 *"I never thought of myself"*   Martha Graham, *Blood Memory: An Autobiography* (New York: Doubleday, 1991), 16.

61 *"the poet knows that he speaks adequately"*   Ralph Waldo Emerson, "The Poet," in *Essays: Second Series* (Boston: Philips, Sampson, 1852), 31.

62 *Artists as diverse*   Questlove, *Creative Quest* (New York: Ecco, 2019), 135; Brian Hiatt, "David Byrne on Trump, Cultural Appropriation and Why He Won't Reunite Talking Heads," *Rolling Stone*, February 1, 2018; Katharine Anne Porter, "The Art of Fiction No. 29," interview by Barbara Thompson Davis, *The Paris Review* 29 (1962): 111; Andy Greene, "Stephen King: The Rolling Stone Interview," *Rolling Stone*, November 6, 2014, 76.

62 *"There are as many kinds of wells"*   Ernest Hemingway, "The Art of Fiction No. 21," interview by George Plimpton, *The Paris Review* 18 (1958).

62 *like Paul Simon, experience themselves as transmitters*   Zollo, *Songwriters on Songwriting*, 120.

67 *"Around 1938, Paul Valery wrote"*   Jorge Luis Borges, *Selected Non-Fictions*, vol. 3 (New York: Penguin, 2000), 240.

68 *"We (the indivisible divinity that works in us)"*   Jorge Luis Borges, "Avatars of the Tortoise," in *Labyrinths* (New York: New Directions, 1962), 208.

68 *"I never completely forget myself"*   Flannery O'Connor, *The Habit of Being: Letters of Flannery O'Connor*, ed. Sally Fitzgerald (New York: Farrar, Straus and Giroux, 1979), 458.

76 *"You dream wonderful things"*   Jeremy Edmiston, from author's notes, January 27, 2013.

78 *both Marlon Brando and Gene Hackman*   Jerry Frebowitz, "*One Flew Over the Cuckoo's Nest*: Ten Things to Know about the Movie," moviefanfare.com, December 8, 2010, https://tinyurl.com/4k4c93dz.

78 *Shaun Tan's frustration*   Shaun Tan, "Shaun Tan in Conversation with Dr. Ric Spencer," *Surburban Odyssey | Exhibition Catalog* (Fremantle, WA: Fremantle Arts Center, 2015), 10.

85 *"objects which in themselves we view with pain"*   Aristotle, *Poetics* 1.4, trans. S. H. Butcher, https://tinyurl.com/6p98czb9.

87 *"And then there is inspiration"*   Graham, *Blood Memory*, 8.

94 *the surrealist photographer Dora Maar*   Amy Crawford, "Finding Dora," *Smithsonian Magazine*, April 2018, 10.

94 *"one's ego is not satisfied by the fact"*   Amy Crawford, "Françoise Gilot Was More Than Picasso's Muse," *Smithsonian Magazine*, April 2022.

96 *"One face looks out from all his canvases"*   Christina Rosetti, "In an Artist's Studio," https://tinyurl.com/2rprepw7.

101 *"The painter, the sculptor, the composer"*   Ralph Waldo Emerson, "The Poet," in *Essays: Second Series*, 42.

101 *"You've got to sell your heart"* Bruccoli, ed., *F. Scott Fitzgerald: A Life in Letters*, 368.

102 *"naked self-expression is the seed of creativity"* Quoted in Lindsey Hilsum, *In Extremis: The Life and Death of War Correspondent Marie Colvin* (New York: Farrar, Straus and Giroux, 2018), 57.

102 *"Rap is thinking out loud"* Jay-Z, "Picasso Baby (A Performance Art Film)," Universal Music Group, 2013.

107 **William Carlos Williams** "William Carlos Williams: Poet and Pediatrician," January 1, 2008, https://tinyurl.com/yn4m9bmb.

107 **Wallace Stevens** "Wallace Stevens, Noted Poet, Dead," *New York Times*, August 3, 1955.

113 *Still, as Stanislavski, the father of Method Acting* Konstantin Stanislavski, *An Actor's Handbook*, ed. and trans. Elizabeth Reynolds Hapgood (Milton Park: Routledge, 2004), 18.

114 *"being at your station"* Quoted in Richard Ford, "Good Raymond," *The New Yorker*, October 5, 1998.

115 *"Is there a word from the Lord?"* Marie Jordan, "An Interview with Li-Young Lee," *AWP Magazine*, May/Summer 2002, https://tinyurl.com/3bn775zn.

115 *"Don't loaf and invite inspiration"* Jack London, "Getting into Print," *Editor*, March 1903, https://tinyurl.com/3ejvta2j.

117 *"out of the work comes the work"* Quoted in Elaine A. King's essay in Harvey Stein, *Artists Observed: Photographs* (New York: Abrams, 1986), 93.

117 *"Inspiration is for amateurs"* Quoted in Mason Currey, *Daily Rituals: How Artists Work* (New York: Alfred A. Knopf, 2013), 64.

117 *"very often ideas occur to me"* Quoted in Laurence Bergreen, *As Thousands Cheer* (New York: Viking, 1996), 121–22.

118 *"square songs," and "round songs,"* Bergreen, *As Thousands Cheer*, 386.

118 *"Which comes first, the words or the music?"* Alan Bunce, "Time after

Time, a Zinger of a Line," *The Christian Science Monitor*, June 14, 1985, https://tinyurl.com/jz8rctt2.

123 **"Talent is insignificant"** Quoted in George Plimpton, ed., *The Writer's Chapbook* (New York: Viking, 1989), 30.

124 **"You're not going to achieve"** Robert Caro, interview with Dave Davies, NPR, April 15, 2019, https://tinyurl.com/bdft6wy9.

125 **"I have had to work hard"** Hans T. David and Arthur Mendel, eds., *The New Bach Reader*, rev. and exp. by Christopher Wolff (New York: Norton, 1999), 20.

126 **Keats left "On First Looking into Chapman's Homer"** Peter Robinson, "On First Looking," in *Poetry and Translation: The Art of the Impossible* (Liverpool: Liverpool University Press, 2010), 1–22.

126 **Rilke wrote the majority of his fifty-five Sonnets to Orpheus** Stephen Mitchell, ed. and trans., *Ahead of All Parting: The Selected Poetry and Prose of Rainer Maria Rilke* (New York: Modern Library, 1995), 575.

126 **Paul McCartney wrote "Yesterday,"** Jordan Zakarian, "Paul McCartney Came Up with the Melody to One of the Beatles' Biggest Hits in His Sleep," September 8, 2020, https://tinyurl.com/4t9sach7.

126 **Lewis Redner woke up with the melody** Ian Bradley, ed., *The Penguin Book of Carols* (New York: Penguin, 1999), 225.

126 **Elvis Costello wrote "The Angels Wanna Wear My Red Shoes"** David Fricke, "Elvis Costello: My Life in Ten Songs," *Rolling Stone*, October 22, 2015.

129 **Erykah Badu freestyled her hit, "Tyrone"** Simon Vozick-Levinson, "Erykah Badu: Born Again," *Rolling Stone*, January 28, 2016, 17–18.

133 **"Thinking should be done beforehand"** Yvonne Baby, "Henri Cartier-Bresson on the Art of Photography," *Harper's Magazine*, November 1961, 74.

151 **most problems can be solved by walking** "Solvitur ambulando," *Merriam-Webster*, https://tinyurl.com/3bk9ewrr.

162 *"there is nothing more truly artistic"* Vincent van Gogh, letter to Theo van Gogh, September 17, 1888, https://tinyurl.com/3c3d38md.

175 *Van Gogh was criticized* "Was Van Gogh Religious?" February 20, 2017, https://tinyurl.com/56xhpd4m.

175 *Tolstoy famously warred with his wife* Alexandra Guzeva, "How Leo Tolstoy Spent His Last Days," *Russia Beyond*, November 20, 2020, https://tinyurl.com/5afatjdy.

175 *American actors and singers marched alongside civil rights leaders* Olivia Hosken, "Celebrities Who Joined the March on Washington," *The Washington Post*, August 19, 2013, https://tinyurl.com/2esx6xf5.

175 *Chinese art students created the Goddess of Liberty statue* Roderick MacFarquhar, *The Politics of China: The Eras of Mao and Deng* (Cambridge: Cambridge University Press, 1997), 455.

175 *Thomas Mapfumo's music* Eric Hansen, "The Lion's Song," January 20, 2012, *Portland Monthly*, February 2012, https://tinyurl.com/4chxerh3.

181 *"lived serenely as an artist greater than all artists"* Vincent van Gogh, *Vincent Van Gogh: Ever Yours; The Essential Letters*, ed. Leo Jansen, Hans Luijten, and Nienke Bakker (New Haven: Yale University Press, 2014), 543.

186 *"inspiration is needed in geometry"* Quoted in Svetlana Evdokimova, *Pushkin's Historical Imagination* (New Haven: Yale University Press, 1999), 19.

186 *The solution to the problem of how to thread the needle* Waldemar Kaempffert, ed., *A Popular History of American Invention*, vol. 2 (New York: Scribner's, 1924), 385.

186 *Russian chemist Dmitri Mendeleev* Paul Strathern, *Mendeleyev's Dream* (New York: Pegasus, 2019), 7.

186 *"An equation for me has no meaning"* Shiyali Ramamrita Ranganathan, *Ramanujan: The Man and the Mathematician* (New Delhi: Ess Ess Publications, 2008), 88.

187 *Every child knows that she can do these things* Brassai and Henry Miller, *Picasso and Company* (Garden City, NY: Doubleday, 1966), 86.

187 ***Vincent van Gogh only sold one painting*** Martin Bailey, "How Did the Only Painting Sold by van Gogh in His Lifetime End Up in Russia?," *The Art Newspaper*, February 4, 2022, https://tinyurl.com/4p3tspsn.

188 ***The year Bach premiered the* St. Matthew Passion** William Mann, *Johann Sebastian Bach: St. Matthew Passion* (London: EMI Records Limited, 1962), 4.